Social Pressures

in

Informal Groups

Social Pressures
in
Informal Groups

A Study of Human Factors in Housing

By

Leon Festinger, Stanley Schachter

and

Kurt Back

STANFORD UNIVERSITY PRESS
STANFORD, CALIFORNIA

Stanford University Press
Stanford, California
Copyright 1950 by Leon Festinger,
Stanley Schachter, and Kurt Back
Printed in the United States of America
First published 1950 by Harper & Brothers
Reissued 1963 by Stanford University Press
Reprinted 1967

Contents

Introduction

SOME time in 1949 I agreed to read a manuscript that was nearing completion. Leon Festinger, then a brand-new colleague, had asked me to give it a critical look; Stanley Schachter and Kurt Back, who had just come with him from Massachusetts Institute of Technology—without Kurt Lewin, alas—were about to finish their doctoral degrees. I wanted, naturally, to see anything that had emerged from their hands, even though I was not prepared to find much excitement in a research monograph which, as I understood it, was devoted to problems of student housing. And so, in a somewhat avuncular mood, I set myself to the task.

Within a few days I had begun what was to become an established habit of quoting from *Social Pressures in Informal Groups*. Sometimes I have wanted to document some of the ways in which person-to-person interaction is dependent upon spatial layout; to this day there remains no better source of evidence than Festinger, Schachter, and Back (1950). Often I have needed to turn to questions of the consequences of differential frequency of interaction: what happens then? Since it was from this book that I first learned about the communicative processes out of which group standards arise, I am still using it as an eye-opener for my students. And, having always admired tight theory construction, I still turn to the margin-scribbled pages of Chapter 9 of my copy of F-S-B. Since it is a gift copy, and autographed, I think I shall continue to use it, dog-ears and all, in spite of my pleasure in seeing this new version at last available.

There is also an important bit of subsequent history to be noted. The work reported in this volume has had that leading-on quality that is so often a touchstone of important research. The authors themselves, as well as all the rest of us, have learned something from it. It was, as I happen to know, one of the direct progenitors of another milestone publication, by the same authors together with H. H. Kelley and J. Thibaut (*Theory and Experiment in Social Communication,* published by the University of Michigan in 1950). Students of the psychological and group conditions of communication, since then, have ignored this work only at their peril. Much of the subsequent work of all these men, and of many of their students (in whose company I like to be included), has been built, directly or indirectly, on *Social Pressures.* What more could one ask of one little book?

Ann Arbor, Michigan   THEODORE M. NEWCOMB
February 1963

Preface

THIS book owes its existence to the generous interest of two separate organizations. The investigations reported here were undertaken at the suggestion and with the financial support of the Albert Farwell Bemis Foundation, established at M.I.T. in 1938 for housing research. They were further continued and carried to completion under contract (N6onr-23212, NR170-698) with the Office of Naval Research.

These sociopsychological studies were originally stimulated by people interested in the field of housing who, though concerned with the immediate practical problems which faced them, felt a keen and continued interest in the work which was primarily on a basic sociopsychological level.

Three persons especially, Burnham Kelly, Robert W. Kennedy, and Catherine Bauer, felt that such basic, theoretical results should become known to people in the field of housing. The authors deeply appreciate their interest, the encouragement and stimulation received from them, and their serious efforts to make these studies of interest to a wider audience.

The authors also wish to thank the numerous people at the Research Center for Group Dynamics who cooperated in various stages of the research, particularly Mr. William Warren and Miss Bobbie Norfleet who ably assisted in the analysis and tabulation of the data; and Mr. Richard Snyder and Mrs. Juliet Brudney who were instrumental in executing the experiment described in Chapter 8. And, of course, we wish to thank the many residents of Westgate and Westgate West for their interest and cooperation.

LEON FESTINGER
STANLEY SCHACHTER
KURT BACK

Social Pressures
in
Informal Groups

Fig. 1. View of Westgate Housing Project, Massachusetts Institute of Technology

1

The Functioning of Groups

SMALL social groups occupy a strategic position as determiners of the behavior and attitudes of their members. Because attitudes and behavior patterns are communicated or learned from other people, it is plausible to suppose that face-to-face communication among members of a social group would be a method through which much of the development of these attitudes and behavior patterns would occur. The type and degree of contact among the members, the functions of the group, and the goals of the group will determine how and why its influences are exerted.

The reasons a small group is able to exercise such influences over its members become clear when we examine the gratifications available only as a result of membership in such a group. Friendships, companionship, and the warmth and pleasures of close emotional ties are, of course, available only as a result of our relationships with other people. Prestige, social status, and the approval of others are in themselves group-oriented goals. They exist only as a particular kind of relationship with other persons. Membership in groups also tends to make accessible to people goals which otherwise would be far out of reach. These goals, whether inherent in the group or incidentally mediated by the group, since they add to the attractiveness of the group, also add to its power. Such strong motivations toward belonging to groups enable the group to have a great deal of influence over its members.

The study of the small group can be a particularly strategic focus in any attempt to understand the influence on the individual of "culture" or of "institutions." If we examine the influence of culture on the behavior of persons the question must be raised as to how these influences are transmitted, maintained, and enforced. Such things as customs and institutionalized patterns of social interaction among people operate somehow to produce a large measure of conformity in people and the problem of the sources of the pressures to conformity and the means of application of such pressures is clearly important. It is likely that there are at least three general sources of such pressure. Some of it undoubtedly comes from within the person himself, who has accepted many values and ideologies during the process of his socialization. Some of the pressures to conform, of course, are exerted on the individual by means of institutions and laws and taboos, rather than by face-to-face communication. These pressures, and how they operate, may be studied by examining the formal structure of a given society. On the other hand, much of the pressure to conformity undoubtedly comes from the smaller groups within a society to which individuals belong. These pressures exist as group standards of the face-to-face group and are only sometimes formalized and made very explicit. Their enforcement depends more on relatively subtle influences and indirect pressures although these are frequently very powerful.

How does the small group function with respect to "sociological variables," such as socioeconomic level, educational level, age, sex, and occupation which are related to a great number of different attitudes?

The formation of face-to-face groups is in part determined by such "sociological variables." Social groups and friendships do form on the basis of common occupation, common sex, residence in the same expensive suburb, or the fact that two people went to the same college or came from the same part of the country. The group, through forming its own standards, affects the formation of attitudes. The actual group memberships, then, in affecting attitude formations, tend incidentally to create uniformities with respect to these sociological variables. It is, therefore, essential to understand the importance of the face-to-face group in order to understand more adequately the importance of the "sociological variables." Of particular relevance would be the study of the effects of these variables on the formation and development of groups.

Emphasis on the importance of the small face-to-face group as a source and mediator of determinants of attitudes and social behavior patterns is not new. The importance of such groups is being stressed more and more in a large variety of problem areas and is being perceived as increasingly important by social practitioners. As a result, there has been an increasing number of studies seeking to understand some of the factors involved in the functioning of small groups and an increasing number of attempts to use such groups in handling applied problems.

The problems of psychotherapy, for example, which have traditionally been regarded as exclusively a matter of treating individual patients, are beginning to be handled by means of group therapy on an experimental basis. In doing therapy with the juvenile delinquent[1, 2, 3] several attempts have been made to treat the group or gang as a whole, rather than to try to change one individual out of context of his group membership. In the treatment of adult behavior disorders efforts have also been made[4, 5, 6] to do intensive psychotherapy with small groups of

[1] Redl, F., "Group Psychological Elements in Discipline Problems." *American Journal Orthopsychiatry,* Vol. 13, pp. 77-82, 1943.

[2] Redl, F., "Diagnostic Group Work." *American Journal Orthopsychiatry,* Vol. 14, pp. 53-67, 1944.

[3] Hogrefe, R., and Harding, J., "Research Considerations in the Study of Street Gangs." (To appear in the *Journal of Applied Anthropology.*)

[4] Frank, J., Personal communication regarding the Veterans' Administration research program in group therapy.

[5] Kelnar, J., "Treatment of Inter-Personal Relations in Groups." *Journal of Social Issues,* Vol. 3, pp. 29-34, 1947.

[6] Strother, C. R., "Methods of Modifying Behavior." *Journal of Social Issues,* Vol. 1, pp. 46-52, 1945.

five to eight patients simultaneously, creating a functioning group rather than a mere collection of individuals. These attempts to change a whole group at once rather than to change individuals are based upon the realization that the group is frequently the anchorage for attitudes and behavior patterns and that the changes produced will be greater and more lasting if a group anchorage for the new attitudes and the new behavior patterns is provided.

The same kinds of theoretical considerations have led to the group treatment of other problems as, for example, retraining foremen in industry[7] or retraining leaders of youth groups.[8] In many instances, as Lewin concluded from his theoretical analysis,[9, 10] it should be easier to change a whole group at once than to change one individual and leave the rest of the group unchanged.

The realization of the importance of the face-to-face group makes it imperative to have a proper formulation of the problems to study and the concepts with which to think. What, then, are the important things to know concerning the face-to-face group which will enable us to understand its functioning and its influences more clearly? We can state some of these problems fairly specifically.

1. How and why are groups formed? The formation of groups is a selective process which is governed by a variety of factors. If a number of people are thrown together for some reason, what

[7] Bradford, L. P., and Lippitt, R., "Role-Playing in Supervisory training." *Personnel*, Vol. 22, pp. 3-14, 1946.

[8] Bavelas, A., "Morale and the Training of Leaders." Chapter VIII, pp. 143-165, in Watson, G. (editor) *Civilian Morale*. New York: Houghton Mifflin, 1942.

[9] Lewin, K., "Frontiers in Group Dynamics: Concept, Method and Reality in Social Science; Social Equilibria and Social Change." *Human Relations*, Vol. 1, pp. 5-41, 1947.

[10] Lewin, K., *Resolving Social Conflicts*. New York: Harper & Brothers, pp. 56-68.

will determine whether or not this collection of people becomes a functioning psychological group? Indeed, what determines whether or not people get thrown together?

When groups form, what are the factors which determine their membership and what determines whether the group lives or dies?

Groups develop along several lines. They develop with respect to membership and size, but they also develop with respect to the activities they engage in, the areas of their members' lives for which they are relevant, and their importance for their members. Some groups are attractive, for example, because they contain many personal friends. Other groups may become important because they help toward some cherished goal such as getting a raise, acquiring prestige, or making it easier to complete a bridge foursome. The problems connected with how groups are held together and how they attract and keep members lead us to another set of questions.

2. How does the group exert influence on its members? There is little doubt that groups have power over their members. They exert influences on their attitudes, on their behavior, and even on the kinds of activities in which their members engage. Questions such as how groups come to have such power and in what ways do they exert it would seem to be very important to answer. What are the factors that are related to the extent of influence which the group can or does exert on its members?

We know that there are many ways in which such influences are exerted. Some groups have verbalized and formalized rules, and institutionalized behaviors to which their members are supposed to conform. Other pressures undoubtedly depend on relatively subtle influences which are exerted during the normal communication process among members of a group. An understanding of the exact workings of this communication process and the way influence is exerted should contribute greatly to an understanding of the strategic position of groups in the lives of their members.

3. How do members resist group induction? Not only are different groups unequally successful in exerting influences on their members, but the same group is not equally successful in influencing different members. Why is it that one person is easily influenced by the group to which he belongs while another person can for a long time successfully resist such influences? How does the group react to the person who successfully resists these influences? Under what circumstances does such a person become a deviate and under what circumstances is he able to influence the other members of the group? When do members or groups of members become differentiated from the rest of the group, resulting in subgroup formation or even exclusion? Because all groups within a given cultural framework do not have the same standards, the deviate must be studied and explained with reference to the particular sources of pressures to conformity which he is able to resist in maintaining his deviate status. A deviate from the culture at large, whose deviate pattern is firmly anchored in a cultural subgroup, may be expected to show different characteristics from a deviate who has no face-to-face group anchorages at all.

Orientation to the way the small face-to-face group functions in the lives of people and the conditions under which this functioning produces one result or another was the basis for the present study. We were able to get answers to some questions and to obtain valuable hints about where to look for answers to others. It may be helpful to describe the general plan of attack which we used and the orientation and reasoning which made one step follow from a preceding one.

In the spring of 1946 a new housing project for married veteran students at the Massachusetts Institute of Technology was ready for occupancy. This housing project, named Westgate, consisted of 100 single-family houses arranged in nine courts. It was located a short distance from the school, and residents moved in according to their order on a waiting list. In July of that same year the present study was started.

Ten months after Westgate was occupied, another housing project, Westgate West, was ready for occupancy. This second housing project was built directly adjoining Westgate and consisted of seventeen former Navy barracks divided into ten apartments per building. The people who moved into this second housing project were also married veterans who were students at the Massachusetts Institute of Technology. They were selected in a manner similar to those in Westgate.

These two new housing projects provided many advantages which promised to help us find answers to some of our questions. There were few prior acquaintances among the residents and the social life of the community had to be built up. We were consequently able to observe, from their beginnings, the formation of social groups and the development of the social processes in which we were interested.

Another feature of these two housing projects made it possible to isolate the relevant variables upon which we wanted to concentrate. If marked differences in background and interest among the residents had existed, these differences might have proved so important as to overwhelm and obscure other determinants of group formation and social process. Here, however, a high degree of similarity existed among the residents, who were all married veteran engineering students.

Field studies such as this one which attempt to describe, quantify, and experiment in the community they investigate, present intriguing methodological problems. The study of anything as complex as the social life of an entire community requires the use of most of the methodological tools available to the social scientist: informants, participant and nonparticipant observation, informal and standardized interviewing, sociometry, and field experimentation. These techniques all supplement one another. They gather data on different aspects of the community way of life. It is only the integration of these diverse data that permits us to piece together a coherent and comprehensive picture of the community under study. A more detailed description and evaluation of the methodology of the present study and a consideration of implications that may be drawn from the methodology of this study to that of other field studies will be presented in the Appendix.

It was encouraging that so many of the aspects of the rich social life which goes on in such a community could be quantified and assembled as hard, conclusive facts. Sometimes these quantitative facts substantiated conclusions that had begun to appear from a qualitative understanding of the lives of these people and sometimes they revealed relationships of which we had no inkling.

After achieving a working knowledge of the kind of people who lived in this project and the type of social life they led, it seemed appropriate, from the point of view of our focus on the functioning of small face-to-face groups, to study the conditions for friendship and group formation within this neighborhood community. Chapter 3 shows that when our data had been assembled, the most striking item was the dependence of friendship formation on the mere physical arrangement of the houses. People who lived close to one another became friendly with each other, while people who lived far apart did not. Mere "accidents" of where a path went or whose doorway a staircase passed were major determinants of who became friends within this community. The small face-to-face social groups which formed were, to a large extent, determined by the fact that a number of people lived in the same apartment building or in the same court. Certainly other factors operated. If two people did not like each other they would not become friends even if they lived right next door to each other. It was impressive, however, to see how large a part mere physical arrangement did play.

After we were able to designate, within this neighborhood community, which social groups existed and which people were members of these social groups, our interest led us to an examination of how membership in these groups affected people's attitudes and behavior. We were fortunate here in being able to study such influences in connection with a new issue which arose in the community.

In the autumn of 1946 the residents of Westgate started to form a tenants' organization. We were able to study the growth of this organization (see Chapter 4) and to observe from the beginning the development of attitudes toward it and of participation in its activities. The fact that the organization would affect equally all subgroups in Westgate and in Westgate West made relevant the investigation of how different group standards had developed in different subgroups and which factors affected the strength and nature of these standards.

Both the qualitative and quantitative data which we gathered in this community pointed clearly to a high degree of uniformity concerning attitudes toward, and activity in, this tenant organization within each of the social groups in Westgate. They also pointed to great differences existing between subgroups in this respect. In Chapter 5 it becomes clear that within each of these small face-to-face groups, group standards had developed concerning this issue. Each group exerted strong influences on its members to conform to its standard. How effectively this influence was exerted on its members depended to a major extent on how cohesive the small social group was. In Chapter 6 we see that, in general, the people who did not conform to the group standard were not as integral a part of the group as those who did.

The clarity of these results and their implication for the functioning of small social groups led us to the formulation of questions which would further clarify understanding. How does the process work by which the group influences its members? Is the communication of such influence a directed process, under what conditions is such influence exerted, and toward whom is the communication directed? The correlated problem deals with the relevance of the structure of a group to such communication and such influence. If the group is constructed so that some people are peripheral members, does that mean that the group communicates less with them and exerts less influence on them?

The tentative answers we were able to obtain to these questions are discussed in Chapter 7. By experimenting on the spread of information in the community we could see some of the factors determining the avenues of communication. We were also able to develop a new method of analyzing the structure of groups and relating this structure to the cohesiveness of the group and the communication pattern within it (Chapter 8).

2

Description of a Housing Community

THIS chapter is a detailed description of the physical plant of the Westgate and Westgate West housing communities and as thorough a treatment as our data permit of the kind of people living in these projects—their backgrounds, interests, attitudes, and present way of life. The design of these projects will be elaborated because, as the next chapter will show, apparently minor features of design are major determinants in the formation of friendships and groups within these two communities.

PHYSICAL CHARACTERISTICS

At the end of the war, the Massachusetts Institute of Technology, like most other universities, had a tremendous increase in its student enrollment. A large part of this increase was made up of returning servicemen, many of whom were married and had children. The housing shortage in the area at the time was particularly acute and the few places that were available rented at figures far above the means of the great majority of these married veteran students. To meet this need the Institute started, in the fall of 1945, to construct two adjoining housing projects with facilities for 270 families. The first of these projects, Westgate, was the first university project in the country for returning married veterans. It was completed some time before the Federal Government started making war housing available to universities.

13

The second project, Westgate West, was built with government aid. The design and construction of these projects were performed under the supervision of architects in the School of Architecture at M.I.T.

These two projects, though located close to M.I.T., were almost completely isolated from any other residential areas. To the north

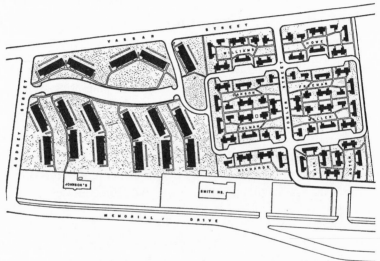

FIG. 2.   Site Plan of Westgate and Westgate West

and west, they were bounded by a solid wall of factories, warehouses, and trucking garages; to the south by a highway and the Charles River; and to the east by athletic fields. One apartment house facing the river was the only other residential building in the area. The nearest shopping district or store of any considerable size was about two miles away and the closest transportation system, a somewhat erratic trolley and bus line, about ⅜ of a mile distant. This relative isolation was a distinct advantage for this study.

The necessarily limited contact and relationship with the larger community meant that these projects could reasonably be considered as self-contained units and study of the interrelations between these projects and the larger community could be minimized.

The first of these projects, Westgate, was completed and fully occupied in the spring of 1946. It was composed of 100 prefabricated, single-family houses. Figure 1 is a photograph of about half of the project; figure 2 is a site plan of the entire project.

As shown in figure 2, the houses are grouped in nine distinct court units which consist of from seven to thirteen houses, arranged in a U-shape. Except for those at the very tips of the U, which face on the street, the houses face on a long, narrow grassy court. The only exception is Richards Court, in the lower left corner of figure 2, which is designed as one half of a U.

The project is divided into two parts by Fowler Street, which runs lengthwise through the middle of the project. The upper six of the nine courts are arranged symmetrically on either side of this street. These courts face one another across Fowler Street and each consists of thirteen houses in identical arrangement. The three lower courts, Richards, Main, and Rotch, all face onto the Charles River. These three smaller courts are made up respectively of seven, seven, and eight houses each.

The houses themselves are one-floor, single-family, wooden prefabs consisting of either two and a half or four rooms. Fifty of these one hundred houses were designed for occupancy by married couples without children. These units consist of a living room with built-in kitchen unit, a bedroom, a bathroom, and a screened-in porch. The other fifty houses were intended for married students with children. These houses are somewhat larger, containing a small extra bedroom and a separate small kitchen. Otherwise all of the houses are identical.

The houses are unfurnished but are provided with a gas-operated, automatic hot water heater and a space heater. The walls are fiberboard finished rather roughly with a single coat of paint.

Rent for the single-bedroom house is $45.00 a month, for the two-bedroom house $55.00 a month. This includes the costs of water, electricity, and garbage and trash removal. It does not include the cost of gas which is used for cooking, hot water heating, and space heating.

The second project, Westgate West, adjoins Westgate and was fully occupied around February, 1947. Westgate West consists of seventeen two-floor, wooden, reconverted Navy barracks. Figure 2 contains a site plan of these buildings.

Each of the buildings is subdivided into ten apartments, five on each floor. Each apartment consists of a kitchen, living room, two bedrooms, and a bath. The layout and construction of each apartment is roughly similar to that of a two-bedroom Westgate house. The apartments differ only slightly from one another in the arrangement and size of rooms. There is a long porch on each floor and the doorway to each of the apartments opens out onto this porch. Thus each floor consists of a row of five directly adjoining apartments whose entrances are about twenty feet apart. A short stairway leads up to each of the lower floor apartments and outside stairways at each end of the lower porch connect the two floors and provide the only paths by which upper-floor residents can reach their floor. All seventeen of the Westgate West buildings are essentially identical.

Some of the Westgate West apartments are partially furnished and rent is approximately $35.00 a month depending upon how much furniture has been supplied. The difference in rent between the two projects exists because Westgate West was government subsidized.

As the courts and buildings were completed they were occupied by applicants on a waiting list operated on a "first come, first served" basis. The only expression of preference permitted was between one- and two-bedroom houses. In filling Westgate West, the top ten applicants moved in as each building was completed. Applicants could express preference for apartment positions, but few did so. Vacancies, as they occur, are filled in order from this same waiting list. Selective influences in assigning particular types of people to particular locations were, therefore, minimal.

Two points concerning these projects are worthy of note:

1. There was no aspect of permanency about living there. The residents all regarded Westgate and Westgate West as places to live only while they were students.

2. There was no long history of residence in these projects. At the time the field experiment was done the oldest resident had been living in Westgate about fifteen months and in Westgate West only five months.

THE PEOPLE OF WESTGATE[1]

Highly selective factors were at work in determining the characteristics of the people who were brought together to live in Westgate. In order to be a resident of Westgate one must have the intelligence, educational background, and interest in technical matters necessary for admission to M.I.T., and the status of

[1] We made our first contact with Westgate in the summer of 1946 when we conducted an interview survey on the sources of satisfaction and dissatisfaction in the Westgate housing project. Forty Westgate housewives, selected at random, were interviewed. These interviews covered a great variety of subjects ranging from specific complaints about minor inconveniences to over-all satisfaction with social life. Much of the material reported in this chapter has been taken from these interviews and from the preliminary research on population characteristics done for these interviews.

Such interviews were not administered to Westgate West since it had not yet been completed. It is probable, however, that all of the major conclusions about Westgate people, their satisfactions and dissatisfactions, and their way of life apply equally well to the people who later moved into Westgate West.

a married veteran. To recognize and identify these areas of homogeneity is important in interpreting the present study, for it is possible that homogeneity per se may have an effect on the functioning of the group. It is possible that had a very hetero-geneous group of people lived in Westgate the community life would have been very different. It is necessary, therefore, to identify specifically the similarities in the Westgate and Westgate West populations.

THE HOMOGENEITY OF THE PEOPLE

1. Homogeneity along Sociological Dimensions. Along the commonly accepted sociological stratifications of class, economic status, age, occupation, education, and marital status, the popu-lations of these two communities exhibited marked homogeneity. We have already mentioned that the residents were all married, veterans, and students at M.I.T. Ages ranged between 20 and 35 with the mean age of the men about 26 and of the women about 24. Within the M.I.T. student body these people represented an older, more mature, and more serious group. In other times, they would have been out of college for several years.

From the limited data on hand, it seems safe to infer that the great majority of the tenants came from upper-middle class homes; ninety per cent came from families who had lived most of their lives in large single-family houses and 65 per cent from homes located in or around cities of over 100,000 population. Eighty-five per cent of the tenants reported that as far back as they could remember their families had lived in only one or two residences.

In contrast to a secure and stable earlier background, these people had recently lived relatively migratory lives due to the demands of military life during the war. Forty-five per cent had lived in more than three different places since their marriage and 50 per cent in from one to three different places.

There was a considerable range of current economic status throughout the projects. Although a few couples enjoyed independent incomes which enabled them to have new cars, fraternity memberships, and similar luxuries, many of them had to struggle to keep within their limited budget. Some 40 per cent of the residents considered themselves financially pressed and everyone had been forced in some way to supplement the $90.00 monthly government allotment. Many of the men worked part time and 27 per cent of the women were employed. Such limited financial resources necessarily meant a very modest scale of living.

Forty per cent of the men had attended M.I.T. before the war. They covered a range of academic progress similar to the rest of the student body, although there was a preponderance of upper-classmen and graduate students (about 25 per cent). The wives of these students had almost all attended college or some kind of professional school.

2. *Homogeneity of Interests.* Because of the fact that M.I.T. is a technical college, the major interests and areas of concentration of these students were focused in scientific and industrial fields. Thus, the great majority of Westgaters took, as their major field of study, one of the engineering or natural sciences. These technical interests were reflected also in leisure-time activities. Those who had the inclination and the time to pursue a hobby seemed to dabble largely in the areas of amateur mechanics, darkroom work, and radio building.

3. *Homogeneity of Aspirations.* Quantitative data on the hopes and ambitions of these people are available only for their future housing aspirations. Thirty-five of the sample of forty who were interviewed stated that they wanted to own their own homes in the near future. Seventy per cent wanted a large house with three or more bedrooms. The general impression one gets is a decided and widespread preference for large, individually owned houses located in or around a large city. Most of the men

anticipated and hoped for successful careers in industry, in which they would climb to positions of major importance.

In summary, the people living in these projects were highly homogeneous along the dimensions of occupation, age, class and family background, education, interests, aspirations, and attitudes toward the community in which they lived. They were an older and more mature group than the general run of students at M.I.T. They probably differed from people living in other similar college housing developments in only one way—their interests were much narrower.

ATTITUDES TOWARD WESTGATE

The strong emphasis in the preceding section on the homogeneities within the Westgate population can be misleading. There were striking individual differences within any group. Even in Westgate, where rigorous selection implies similarities in educational background, age, interests, and occupation, there were no selective influences at work on personality, popularity, sociability, political attitudes, and so on. We can reasonably expect, then, that some of these people would love living in Westgate while others would dislike it; some would be social lions and others relatively isolated; and some would think the tenants' organization a wonderful idea, while others would have no use for it. To illustrate the extent of these differences and to reveal the general pattern of life in Westgate, we have selected passages from two interviews which differ along lines pertinent to this study.

The first interview came from a sociable girl who liked her house and particularly liked the social life afforded by Westgate. She made many minor complaints but these were all half-whimsical suggestions for the improvement of a place she liked despite its faults.

(*Reasons for coming to Westgate and anticipations about it*)   My husband wanted to come back to school and, being able to find no other place, we came here. To tell the truth, I hadn't any idea what it would be like living here. I thought it would be fun to live in a community like this. As far as the house was concerned, I didn't see anything but diagrams. It's the first place of our own, so we're thrilled about it. What I did like was the idea of having a place of our own and a room of her own for the baby. She'd never had that before. Oh, *one* thing I thought I wouldn't like—having no tub. That irked me terribly.

(*Realization of anticipations*)   About the unpleasantness of not having a tub—I just use a galvanized tub and that's a riot, it's really funny getting that in the shower. The houses may be expensive but that's just one of those things. One thing, the kitchen unit to me is simply *ideal*. It's small but very handy and I've had no trouble with it at all.

(*Previous housing experience*)   I've lived in mother's home in Buffalo—a great big house very close to the city. When George was in the service, we lived in rooms and shabby apartments in Arkansas and Missouri.

(*Difficulties in leaving Westgate*)   I really think it's going to be difficult for we've made friends—it's like a community—I think we'll never again have a chance to live in a place like this where everyone has the same interest and everyone is so friendly.

(*Difficulties involved for Westgate women holding a job*)   Well, I don't work but I would like to. The greatest problem I've heard about from the working girls is shopping. I don't know what else—of course, trying to get their housework done. For those who'd be willing to leave their children and go to work, it would be wonderful if Tech would set up a nursery.

(*Friends inside and outside of Westgate*)   I don't have any friends here in Boston, I only know people in Westgate. Mostly I know the people in this court—about twenty all together—of course, I know some better than others. I don't think living here limits your friendships, certainly not if you can become acquainted with everybody here. I don't feel I have much chance to meet others for there's a limit on outside contacts but I really don't feel any need for friends outside of Westgate.

(*Comparison with living quarters of non-Westgate friends*)   Most of my other married friends live in the ———— University housing project which is much inferior to this. I saw it on my vacation last summer and it can't even compare. Others are living at home with their parents and trying to find a place. We're really very fortunate.

(*Membership in organizations outside of Westgate*)   I don't belong to any, I'm sorry to say. I just haven't been able to. I wanted to attend the M.I.T. Dames, but the meetings aren't at a convenient time. We haven't even attended any of the M.I.T. social functions—we haven't been anywhere. It doesn't seem that Westgaters have as much to do with M.I.T. activities as other M.I.T. married students. I feel most of the people living here are quite satisfied and find their activities inside of Westgate.

I have a wonderful idea on that subject. I feel we need an organization. Also we ought to have a little place for the girls to gather in the evenings so we don't have to sit here, not saying a word while our husbands study. Just sit! Very few of us know outside friends and we can't invite Westgate friends in while our husbands study. There's a little house down here, an office, and I've never seen anyone in it except when we signed the leases. I've had my eye on that for some time. If we had an organization at Westgate it might have results on getting up a little place.

(*Community activities in Westgate*)   I think that to start any activities like these we would have to have an organization to present plans to the group at Tech—an organization in order to show that more than two or three people were interested or they wouldn't go to so much trouble. So many of the people I've talked to in this neighborhood think it's a joke. A few think it's a good idea but no one has been able to get right at it.

In a place like Westgate it's easy to have community activities because of the fact that we all get to know each other so well, we all have common grounds. It's not like in a suburb where strangers come in and there are cliques. We're all living under the same conditions and that has a great deal to do with bringing people together.

(*Contacts with neighbors*)   Oh—during the day we keep running in and out of the houses—for no excuses, for no reasons, my husband says it's just like living in a dormitory. Then bridge in the evenings—some place close so I can listen to the baby. Since we don't have any friends outside of Westgate we can't invite them to our home but, of course, we invite our Westgate friends in all the time.

(*Opinions about the management*)   One thing the management did that struck such an important note with the girls was the seeding of the grass. It's just now beginning to look like grass.

If they'd fix the leaky roofs it would be a joy. That's the bane of my existence in this kind of weather. There are two or three leaks in the bathroom, several in the kitchen, and it runs down the walls in the living room.

What could an organization do? As one of my friends suggested, if they don't cut the grass, we could complain as a group; and maybe we could even get the roofs fixed up sooner if we did that. I think a lot could be accomplished by organizing—recreation, nursery, getting things done. The management has been very good but some girls are still lacking pieces in their refrigerators and have iceboxes. Maybe it's not the fault of Tech, but production.

(*Best number of families to have in project of this sort; privacy*) The project being spaced the way it is, I don't see that it makes very much difference how many live here. If the houses were all in a circle it would be different, but the way it is, everyone gets acquainted with the people in their own court.

We feel we have a good deal more privacy than some people here, for at night we're not bothered by people coming around—that's the advantage of the houses at this end of the project.

(*Inconveniences due to size and arrangement of rooms*)   It would be wonderful if George had some other room to study in—that especially. The only thing I can think of is having him study in the bedroom but he doesn't like that—so I go into the bedroom when I have visitors.

(*Would you move?*)   No, I don't think we'd ever be as happy living in an apartment. Most likely we'd be surrounded by people with all different ages and interests. Here we're all the same age and all of us are here for one purpose and our interests are so much alike.

The second interview came from a person in very different circumstances and with distinctly different attitudes toward life in Westgate. This girl worked, had no children, and anticipated living in Westgate only one year more.

(*Reasons for coming to Westgate and anticipations about it*) We really didn't want to but we couldn't find an apartment of any kind. We were living in just one room. We were very skeptical about it—very, very. The thing we were most leery of was the heating—and we still are. I detest houses with no foundation—I'm afraid we will have rats, although we haven't yet. Our primary reason for not wanting to move in was that my husband was familiar with projects of this type. What I was especially interested in was the surroundings —the people. I expected to find the people interesting.

(*Realization of anticipations*) The heater is still one of the disadvantages. It just doesn't suffice. As for the people, yes, I found them about as I expected. They are usually friendly—they all have the same problems.

(*Previous housing experience*) Before this in Cambridge—one room and that very bad. It was very difficult for me to sleep where Ron was studying. While Ron was overseas I lived in New Hampshire with my parents. Our last home together was a three-room apartment in Norfolk near the base. It was very spacious and nice. Before that we lived in New York—before Ron went into the service that is. We had a four-room apartment in Malvern, Long Island—definitely a residential area.

(*Difficulties in leaving Westgate*) It won't be hard at all. We really don't have any roots here at all—no family around. The only ties we have at all are the fact that my husband is here in school and that our furniture is here.

(*Difficulties involved for Westgate women holding a job*) Well, I work as secretary to an insurance man and the only great difficulty I have is shopping—no others. I imagine you would have the same problem anywhere. I always have, at least.

(*Friends inside and outside of Westgate*) We know few people except in Westgate—the majority of our friends live here. Living here limits your friendships because you don't look beyond Westgate, but we don't particularly feel a need for any outside friends. We haven't even kept up contact with the few friends we do have outside.

(*Comparison with living quarters of non-Westgate friends*) I think Westgate is better than the places our M.I.T. friends are living in. The majority of those we know outside want to get in here, they were very much interested in it. But Westgate can't compare to the places in which our non-M.I.T. friends live. The majority of them have much larger and more comfortable quarters.

(*Membership in organizations outside of Westgate*)   I don't do anything but Ron is very active in the Aeronautical Society. We haven't gone to any M.I.T. social functions except a few that the Aeronautical Society has arranged.

(*Community activities in Westgate*)   It would be hard for anyone who works to talk about that. I just don't have the time. I presume those girls who stay at home would like bridge clubs and teas occasionally. I imagine things like this would serve to bring the wives together especially. I don't know anyone outside this court. Boys seem to get around and know more people. One of the difficulties involved in having community activities I guess is that there is no central meeting place such as an auditorium.

(*Contacts with neighbors*)   I see them on week ends. The minute we go out on the porch we seem to have a following. I certainly don't see them to borrow. The gardens tend to bring the boys together. They compare tomato plants and have a wonderful time.

We quite often have Westgate class friends of my husband's and their wives for dinner and to listen to records. When the wives are gone we have the husbands in to meals. We have asked our non-Westgate friends in too. We do the usual things—eat, drink, etc.

(*Opinions about the management*)   My only contact with them is when we have a complaint, but I certainly don't think they respond to complaints! I think they show a total lack of interest.

What could an organization do? I feel that if the majority got up a list of complaints and took them to someone at Tech we would get better response. The agents give the feeling that they are much too busy to be bothered with Westgate. Many of us have been very neatly pushed by them whereas Tech has a definite interest here and would be much different about it. If an organization were formed we definitely would get better action.

(*Best number of families to have in project of this sort; privacy*) As small a group as possible rather than larger. That would give quite a bit more outside space and privacy if there weren't so many houses on this one plot of ground. We like the privacy. It is a lot easier to study—all we have to do is close the door and everyone knows he is studying and goes away.

(*Inconveniences due to size and arrangement of rooms*)   There is a definite disadvantage in the bedroom. We have twin beds and with them there is no room for turning around in the bedroom. The living room could be larger too. If we had been smart, we would have

gotten a double house and my husband would have had a study.
(*Would you move?*) No—we only have another year here—
definitely not. But if we were going to be here for two years we would
look for a larger place. Of course it couldn't be more ideally located
for both of us because I work just about three blocks on the other
side of the railroad track.

These interviews have been selected because they represent
polar attitudes toward Westgate. The more negative person felt
that there was a lot wrong with the place, but it was not too bad
since it was only temporary. The favorable girl made a few suggestions for improvement but was delighted with almost everything about the project. One is struck by the fact that despite
these interviews representing the extremes of reactions to Westgate, the differences between them on most matters is slight. The
indications of similarity in attitudes and pattern of social life in
Westgate is supported by the data presented below.

The discussion of these two interviews has illustrated a number
of variables significant for this study. An accurate picture of this
community, however, demands that we present data for the
entire group of Westgate interviewees.

Over-all Satisfaction.   Responses to the question, "How do you
like your present home?" break down as follows:

We love it, it's very nice, etc.	75%
Satisfactory for the present	25%

No one openly disliked his present home. The range of satisfaction, therefore, extended from a neutral position to a high level
of general satisfaction, and the majority of Westgaters were quite
pleased with their homes.

The following reasons were given in response to "why" (do
you like or dislike your present home?). These figures add to
more than 100 per cent because many people gave several
reasons.

Favorable Responses

It's our own home	28%
Congenial community	25%
We have privacy and freedom	22%
Easy to take care of	22%
Convenient to Tech	20%

Unfavorable Responses

Specific physical complaints:	
roof leaks, heating, etc.	20%
It's too small	10%

It is apparent that there were relatively few unfavorable comments about the Westgate homes. Those which did occur concerned themselves with the smallness of the home and with a miscellany of physical complaints. The two physical aspects of the Westgate homes which were mentioned as favorable characteristics were the convenience to M.I.T. and the ease with which the house could be taken care of. The most frequently mentioned items, however, did not concern physical characteristics at all. They concerned feelings about its being "their own home," privacy and freedom, and the congeniality of the other residents. It seems likely that it was these nonphysical aspects of living in Westgate that contributed most to the almost uniform satisfaction which existed.

Comparative Advantages. Another way of looking at the satisfactions of the Westgate residents is to obtain a comparison between their living quarters and those of their friends who did not live in Westgate. Responses to the question, "How do your living quarters compare to those of other married friends of yours?" follows:

Westgate is better	60%
Some have better places and others worse	15%
No opinion	25%

Here again, the range of opinion was from neutral to favorable, with no instances of opinions which were entirely unfavorable. The majority felt that they were better off than others they knew who lived elsewhere.

Specific Complaints. At various points throughout the interviews there were opportunities to express specific sources of dissatisfaction. The following tabulation presents the specific complaints about Westgate.

Lack of laundry facilities	63%
Difficult to heat	72%
Too much dust	72%
Smell from factories	48%
Houses too small	37%
Leaking roofs	28%
Sinks too small	18%

The complaints concerned recognized physical inadequacies of Westgate and were generally mentioned by a large number of people. No complaints were made about neighbors or the social life in the project.

Social Satisfaction. Specific satisfaction with social life within Westgate was widespread. There was a general realization that Westgate housed a congenial group of people and most agreed that Westgate community life adequately satisfied their social needs.

Responses to the question, "Do you feel that living in Westgate limits or enlarges your friendship?" were:

Enlarges because there are so many of us living together	40%
Enlarges because it is a congenial community with everyone in the same boat	35%
It limits friendship	15%
No difference	10%

Three-fourths of the residents of Westgate perceived that living in the project enlarged their opportunities to make friends. The reasons given were the same ones mentioned as contributing to their satisfaction. The congeniality of the other people in Westgate, and the fact that they were all "in the same boat" made it easy to make friends. Only 15 per cent of the people felt that the isolation of Westgate was a limitation on the friendships which they otherwise might have been able to make. The friendships which did arise seemed to be active social relationships, for 80 per cent of the people said that they invited other Westgaters to their homes frequently.

For most Westgaters these friendships within the community apparently constituted a satisfactory social life. The two following sets of data indicate that Westgaters had few social contacts or activities outside of their own community and apparently felt little need for such contacts. The question, "What organizations and groups (churches, etc.) have you joined at M.I.T. and elsewhere around here?" elicited these responses:

No organizations	50%
M.I.T. Dames (a student and faculty wives' group)	30%
Organizations outside of M.I.T.	20%

When the few who said they were members of some group were asked, "How active are you in these organizations?" 85 per cent replied that they were not active at all. Thus, only the smallest handful of Westgaters took any sort of active part in any organization outside of Westgate.

Moreover, they apparently felt little need for any friends outside of the project itself. In response to the question, "Do you feel a need for friends outside of Westgate?" they replied:

No	75%
Yes	15%
It is always nice to have more friends	10%

The picture emerges that Westgate was socially a self-contained community. Because of the homogeneous and congenial group living there, it was a simple matter to strike up friendships. These relationships within the project were evidently gratifying, for the great majority of these people felt no need for any outside activities or friendships.

THE KIND OF LIFE THEY LED

The combination of circumstances in which these people found themselves—the isolation of the community, their relative maturity in the college community, the absorption in study, the large proportion of families who had small children, generally meager financial resources, and congenial neighbors—made for a modest, though pleasant, manner of life within the community. Each of these factors, however, imposed sharp limitations on freedom of movement. Student status, for example, necessarily meant that the major portion of the husband's time was taken up with attending classes and studying. Some of these limitations are revealed in the responses to the question, "What particular problems arise from the fact that your husband is a student?"

Husband too busy for social activities	75%
Financial problems	48%
Must be quiet while husband studies	28%
No time for companionship with husband	18%
Husband needs separate study	15%

Being a student restricted social activity and even limited interaction between husband and wife. Leisure-time activities were similarly restricted by limited finances or having to look after the baby. When asked, "Where do you prefer to spend your leisure time?" most Westgaters replied, "At home." Indeed, social life seems to have been encompassed by an occasional movie, exchanging dinners with the neighbors, asking one's court neighbors in to chat, and playing bridge. In addition, the physical isolation of the project and the maturity of Westgaters relative to their college classmates sharply limited contact between Westgate and the rest of the college or the Boston community. This combination of circumstances plus the fact that Westgaters found one another so congenial a group made this community the center around which the social lives of almost all its residents revolved.

Within Westgate, the social unit was the court. For a variety of reasons which will be discussed in the next chapter, the people living in each court knew each other better and spent more time with one another than with anyone else in the project. This meant, of course, that most of each resident's friends were concentrated in his own court and consequently most of his social activity centered around his own court. Thus, one's court neighbors were the people with whom one shopped, walked to school, played bridge, and generally saw most often just for chatting and general cooperation. Court parties were frequent and during the summer several courts held picnics in their courtyards.

Summary

It was suggested earlier that it is necessary to study the homogeneity of the members of a group in order to fully understand the group. The degree of homogeneity in and of itself may seriously affect the functioning and pattern of life of the group. This point can now be more specifically formulated.

There is abundant evidence that the high degree of homogeneity among the Westgate residents promoted a congenial social atmosphere. That there was general satisfaction with social life within Westgate has been pointed out. Two facts are clear. First, Westgate people did have the feeling that Westgate promoted friendships and seemed to be satisfied with the friendships they developed. Secondly, there was high dependence upon Westgate for these friendships and little going outside of the project for social activities. The most frequently expressed explanation of this high level of social satisfaction was that "Westgate is such a congenial community, everybody is the same age and has the same interests and is leading the same kind of life you are." The hypothesis may therefore be advanced that in such a housing community homogeneity promotes satisfactory social life.

In the next chapter emphasis will be placed on the ecological determinants of group structure. We will see that within the Westgate community the ecological factors of distance and position were major determinants of group formation. Stress has been laid on the homogeneity of the Westgate population because of the possibility that these ecological factors take on major importance only in a homogeneous community. In a community where most of the people are alike and probably all congenial to one another, friendships are probably far more likely to spring up on the basis of these ecological factors than they are in a heterogeneous community.

3

The Spatial Ecology of Group
Formation

HUMAN ecology has dealt mainly with the study of the distribution of persons, institutions, or any social phenomena in space.
Among the concerns of the human ecologist have been studies of
the spatial distribution and patterning of such things as delin-
quency, truancy, crime, vice, suicide, mental disorders, divorce,
desertion, poverty, mortality, etc. Almost without exception these
studies have followed a common pattern—a relatively large area,
such as a metropolitan region, is subdivided into a number of
zones or enumeration districts in each of which the rate of
occurrence of a particular social phenomenon is computed. Little
attention has been devoted to the possible effects of the spatial
arrangement of smaller areas such as neighborhoods, nor has
attention been focused on the relations between ecological factors
and the formation of friendship and face-to-face groups.

Stouffer[1] in a study of mobility says, "Whether one is seeking
to explain 'why' persons go to a particular place to get jobs, 'why'
they go to trade at a particular store, 'why' they go to a particular neighborhood to commit a crime, or 'why' they marry the
particular spouse they choose, the factor of spatial distance is of
obvious significance."

Direct research on the ecological determinants of friendship

[1] Stouffer, S. A., "Intervening Opportunities: A Theory Relating
Mobility and Distance." *American Sociological Review*, Vol. 5, pp. 845-867,
1940.

and group formation has, however, been minimal. A few studies [2, 3] have examined the relationship between distance and marriage selection. Such studies show that there is an inverse relationship between the distance separating potential marriage partners and the number of marriages. Thus, in New Haven, 76 per cent of the marriages in 1940 were between persons living within twenty blocks of each other and 35 per cent between persons living within five blocks of each other.[3]

While such findings may not seem surprising, it is less obvious that differences in distance as small as twenty or thirty feet would play a major part in determining friendships. Within the Westgate and Westgate West housing projects, however, even these small differences in distance are effective in determining patterns of friendship. This chapter outlines the relationships between the physical environment and the sociometric structure of these two communities.

The Ecological Bases of Friendship

In communities such as Westgate or Westgate West, where people moving into the area have few or no previous contacts in the community, friendships are likely to develop on the basis of the brief and passive contacts made going to and from home or walking about the neighborhood. These brief meetings, if they are frequent enough, may develop into nodding acquaintanceships, then into speaking relationships, and eventually, if psychological factors are right, into friendships. Such casual or involuntary meetings we will call passive contacts.

Passive contacts are determined by the required paths followed in entering or leaving one's home for any purpose. For example, in going from one's door to the stairway one must pass certain

[2] Abrams, R. H., "Residential Propinquity as a Factor in Marriage Selection." *American Sociological Review*, Vol. 8, pp. 288-294, 1943.

[3] Kennedy, R., "Premarital Residential Propinquity." *American Journal of Sociology*, Vol. 48, pp. 580-584, 1943.

apartments; in walking to the butcher shop one must go by certain houses. These specific required paths are determined by the physical structure of the area.

In relating physical structure to the formation of friendships, it is necessary to distinguish between two ecological factors, (1) physical distance, and (2) positional relationships and features of design which we may call functional distance.

1. Physical distance is measured distance and is one of the major determinants of whether or not passive contacts will occur. Obviously there is a high negative relationship between the physical distance separating the homes of two people and the probability that these people will make passive contact. The smaller the physical distance the greater the number of required paths neighbors are likely to share and the greater the probability of passive contacts. For example, in hanging clothes out to dry, or putting out the garbage, or simply sitting on the porch one is much more likely to meet next-door neighbors than people living four or five houses away.

2. Factors such as the design of a building or the positional relationships among a group of houses are also important determinants of which people will become friends. It is these functional factors of design and position which determine the specific pattern of required paths in an area and consequently determine which people will meet. For example, if there is a stairway at each end of a floor, there is a good chance that people living at opposite ends of the floor will never or rarely meet. Functional distance is measured by the number of passive contacts that position and design encourage.

Both physical distance and functional distance, therefore, will affect the pattern and number of passive contacts. Obviously, they cannot be considered as independent variables, for we can expect a high relationship between the two. In particular cases, however, the distinction becomes clear. For example, two back-to-back houses which are thirty feet apart and have neither back doors nor back yards would be considered functionally farther apart than two back-to-back houses, also thirty feet apart, which do have back doors and yards. Thus we can have varying functional distances while physical distance remains constant.

THE EFFECT OF PHYSICAL DISTANCE ON THE
FORMATION OF FRIENDSHIPS

Figure 3 is a schematized representation of the front of a Westgate West building. The porch area provides the only means of entering or leaving the building and is, therefore, the only

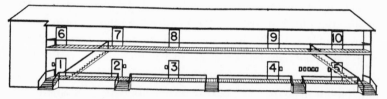

Fig. 3.   Schematic Diagram of a Westgate West Building

place within the building in which passive contacts can occur. Each of the doorways is the entrance to a different apartment and the numbers on the doorways will be used to designate each apartment position. Each floor consists of five directly adjoining apartments and the two floors are connected by stairways at each end of the porch. With two exceptions the doorways of all adjoining apartments are separated by almost 19 feet. Apartments 3 and 4 and apartments 8 and 9 are separated by 32 feet. The maximum separation on any one floor is the 88 feet between the end apartments.

In order to simplify the presentation of data we have adopted a unit of approximate physical distance to describe the difference between any two apartments in a building. Each unit is the equivalent of the physical distance separating any two neighboring doorways. Thus, in Figure 3, apartments 1 and 2 are one unit of approximate physical distance apart; apartments 1 and 3 are two units apart; apartments 1 and 5 and apartments 6 and 10 are four units apart, and so on. In specifying the distance between apartments on different floors, the letter S is employed as a symbol for the stairways between the first and second floors. Thus, apartments 9 and 1 are separated by two units of physical distance and a stairway and this distance is designated as 2S; apartments 2 and 7 are separated by 1 unit and a stairway and are 1S units apart, and so on. Despite the fact that the stairway on the right-hand side of the building ends midway between apartments 9 and 10, the units are calculated as if this stairway ended right in front of the door of apartment number 9. This procedure has been adopted for simplicity's sake and makes little difference in our results. Where there are two possible routes connecting any apartment on one floor to any apartment on the other floor, the units are always computed for the shorter route.

In order to study the effect of these physical design features on the formation of friendships we may relate such things as physical distance to sociometric choices. These sociometric data were gathered on all residents of Westgate and 166 of the 170 Westgate West residents by asking, "What three people in Westgate or Westgate West do you see most of socially?"

Table 1 presents the data for Westgate West on choices given to people living in the same building and on the same floor as the person who chooses them. The data for all seventeen Westgate West buildings are grouped since all of these buildings are exactly the same.

In column (1) of Table 1 are listed all the approximate physical distances which can separate any two persons living on the same floor. Column (2) presents the total number of choices given to persons living at each distance away from the people who are choosing. These figures, however, are inadequate in this form because there are great differences in the total number of potential choices between people separated by the various distances. There are, for example, many more 1 unit choices than 4 unit choices possible. These figures in column (2) must, consequently, be corrected on the basis of the total number of such possible choices.

Table 1.—The Relationship Between Sociometric Choice and Physical Distance on One Floor of a Westgate West Building

(1)	(2)	(3)	(4)
Units of approximate physical distance	Total number of choices given	Total number of possible choices	Choices given (2) ⁄ Possible choices (3)
1	112	8×34	.412
2	46	6×34	.225
3	22	4×34	.162
4	7	2×34	.103

Column (3) presents the correction factors for each distance of separation between apartments. The figures in this column represent the total number of choices that could exist in the entire Westgate West project at each separation distance. Thus, at three units distance, there are four possible choices within any one floor; apartments 4 to 1, 5 to 2, 1 to 4, and 2 to 5 on the first floor or, symmetrically, apartments 9 to 6, 10 to 7, 6 to 9, and 7 to 10 on the second floor. Since there are seventeen buildings, each with two floors, the number of possible choices at each distance is multiplied by thirty-four. Column (4) presents the corrected sociometric choices at each distance. These figures are arrived at by dividing the figures in column (2) by those in column (3). They state specifically the percentage of possible choices at each distance that were actually made. Thus, 41.2 per cent of the 272 possible one unit choices were actually made; 22.5 per cent of the 204 possible two unit choices were made.

The data in Table 1 show unequivocally that within the floor of a Westgate West building there is a high relationship between friendships and physical distance. The greatest percentage of possible choices are made to next-door neighbors. These percentages decrease constantly with distance to a minimum of 10.3 per cent of all choices that could be exchanged between people four units apart, that is, between those who live at opposite ends of the same floor. It must be remembered that these distances are actually small. Neighboring apartments are about 22 feet apart and apartments at opposite ends of the same floor are only 88 feet apart. Yet these small differences in distance seem to be major determinants of whether or not friendships will form.

These choices given to people living on the same floor represent a very sizeable proportion of the total number of choices given. Forty-four per cent of the 426 choices made were given to people living on the same floor as the chooser.

We find a similar relationship of sociometric choice to physical distance in choices given to people living in the same building but on a different floor. Table 2 presents data for between-floor choices. The meaning of each of the columns is the same as in Table 1. The letter S in column (1) is the symbol for stairway.

The data in Table 2 show a high relationship between choices exchanged among people living on different floors of the same barracks and the distance between these people. Again, those people having the smallest physical separation give each other the highest proportion of the total number of possible choices. Thus, 20.6 per cent of the 68 possible choices are made at S units, the shortest possible distance between apartments on different floors. These percentages decrease constantly with increasing distance to a low point of 5.9 per cent of possible choices between apartments with a separation of 3S or 4S units of approximate physical distance.

Table 2.—The Relationship of Sociometric Choices Between Floors of a Westgate West Building to Physical Distance

(1)	(2)	(3)	(4)
Units of approximate physical distance	Total number of choices given	Total number of possible choices	Choices given (2) / Possible choices (3)
S	14	2×34	.206
1S	39	6×34	.191
2S	20	8×34	.074
3S	14	7×34	.059
4S	4	2×34	.059

Whereas 44 per cent of the total number of sociometric choices in Westgate West were made to others on their own floor, only 21 per cent of the total choices were made between floors.

The data in columns (4) of Tables 1 and 2 are presented graphically in Figure 4. This figure plots the percentage of the total possible choices made at each approximate physical distance for choices within the same floor and choices between floors. Both curves are monotonically decreasing curves.

Though both curves decrease there are differences between them. The curve for same-floor choices drops sharply from point to point. The first two points of the curve for between-floor choices are at about the same level. The curve then drops and the next three points again are all at about the same low level. Both curves are, in part, affected by functional factors but positional relationships have played so strong a part in shaping the between-floor curve that it may well be considered more a curve of functional than of physical distance.

Data on the effects of physical distance on friendship formation are more difficult to obtain for Westgate. Within any one court there are houses next to one another and houses facing one another. Some of the back-to-back houses have back doors while others do not, and so on. Even if one wishes to ignore the possible

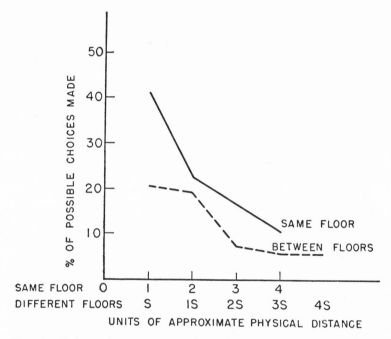

FIG. 4. Relationship Between Physical Distance and Sociometric Choices in Westgate West

effects of different functional relationships throughout this community, it would be almost impossible to compute the relationship of physical distance per se to friendship formation because of the extreme difficulty of determining the necessary correction factors for the number of possible choices at various distances.

However, for part of each side of a large Westgate U-shaped court it is possible partially to isolate the effect of physical distance. Figure 5 is a schematic representation of any pair of the six identically designed courts which face one another across the street dividing the project in two (see Figure 2). Each of the letters in Figure 5 represents a different house. The houses

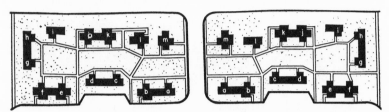

FIG. 5.   Schematic Diagram of the Arrangement of the Westgate Court

lettered *b, c, d, e, f,* and those lettered *l, k, j, i, h* are approximately arranged in rows and are somewhat similar in this respect to the five apartments on each floor of a Westgate West building. The end houses *a* and *m* are not included in this grouping because they face onto the street whereas all of the other houses in the row face into the courtyard.

Analysis of the sociometric choices exchanged among the people living in each row of houses follows the same pattern as the analysis of choices among apartments on the same floor of a Westgate West building. Distance between houses is again handled in terms of units of approximate physical distance. Thus, *b* is separated from *c* by one unit, from *d* by two units, and so on. The average measured distance between houses is about 45 feet. Choices are again categorized according to the units of distance separating the house of the person chosen from that of the person choosing. The data for all twelve rows are pooled and are presented in Table 3. Again, there is the same marked relationship between sociometric choice and physical distance. The greatest proportion of possible choices is made to next-door neighbors.

This proportion decreases with increasing distance to the low point of no choices at all to people living four units away.

These data are presented graphically in Figure 6. The curve is similar to the one obtained for choices within one floor of a Westgate West building.

Table 3.—The Relationship of Sociometric Choices Among the Houses in a Row in Westgate Courts to Physical Distance

(1)	(2)	(3)	(4)
Units of approximate physical distance	Total number of choices given	Total number of possible choices	Choices given (2) / Possible choices (3)
1	26	8×12	.271
2	6	6×12	.083
3	2	4×12	.042
4	0	2×12	.000

In summary, data for two differently designed housing projects show a strong relationship between sociometric choice and physical distance. In both projects the greatest number of choices were made to people living closest to the person choosing and the choices decreased continuously as distance from the home of the chooser increased. The actual measured distances involved were quite small, in no case being larger than 180 feet. Yet the effect of even these small distances is so marked that in a Westgate row no choices at all were made between houses with the maximum separation of four units or 180 feet.

THE EFFECT OF PHYSICAL DISTANCE ON CHOICES
OUTSIDE OF OWN COURT OR BUILDING

The data presented so far have explored the relationships between sociometric choices and physical distances within a court or building. This same relationship holds for choices outside

of the court or building. The greater the physical separation
between any two points in these communities, the fewer the
friendships. Table 4 presents the data for choices given by Westgaters to people living anywhere in the two projects. Column (1)
lists the places of residence of the people chosen. "Own court"

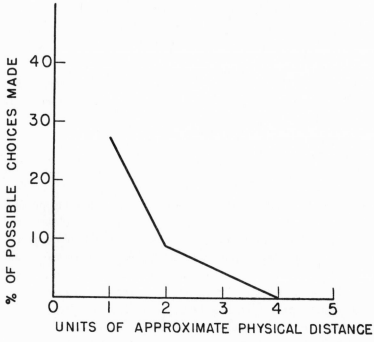

FIG. 6.   Relationship Between Physical Distance and Sociometric
Choices Along Each Side of the Westgate Courts

refers to a choice made within the court of the chooser; "adjacent
court" refers to choices given to people living in immediately
neighboring courts. "Other courts" refers to any choice within
Westgate which does not fall into the first two categories. "Westgate West" includes all choices given by Westgaters to people

in Westgate West. In the order given, these categories approximate a continuum of physical distance. In general, though not in all cases, "own court" choices are physically closer than "adjacent court" choices and so on.

Table 4.—Sociometric Choices Given by Westgaters to People Living Anywhere in the Two Projects

(1)	(2)	(3)	(4)
Location of person chosen	Total number of choices	Total number of possibilities	Choices given (2) / Possible choices (3)
Own court	143	1076	.133
Adjacent court	51	2016	.025
Other courts	47	6794	.007
Westgate West	17	17,000	.001

Table 4 makes it obvious that the relationship between physical distance and sociometric choice holds for out-of-court choices as well as in-court choices. Column (4) again shows that the percentage of possible choices made decreases with increasing distance.

The data for Westgate West presents a similar picture. Table 5 shows that for Westgate West, too, there is an inverse relation-

Table 5.—Sociometric Choices Given by Westgate West People to People Living Anywhere in the Two Projects

(1)	(2)	(3)	(4)
Location of person chosen	Total number of choices made	Total number of possibilities	Choices given (2) / Possible choices (3)
Own buildings	278	1530	.182
Own quadrangle	49	4000	.012
Other buildings	66	23,200	.003
Westgate	33	17,000	.002

ship between the percentage of possible choices actually made and physical distance.

In describing the six large Westgate courts we mentioned that, with the exception of the end houses at the tips of the U, all of the houses constituting a court face into the courtyard area. All but two of these end houses face out onto the street which runs through the project. In Figure 2, such houses would be numbers 8 and 20 in Tolman court, 21 and 33 in Carson court, and so on. The only exceptions are number 34 in Williams and 59 in Howe. These two end houses face into the courtyard.

Because of these differences in position we can expect marked functional differences between these end houses and the rest of the houses in the court. It is possible to come and go from the end houses facing the street without ever passing the homes of court neighbors. One can work in the garden or sit out on the porch and only rarely meet court neighbors. None of these things are true for the houses facing into the court. Therefore, we can expect that the people living in the end houses facing the street will have far fewer passive contacts with their court neighbors than will people living in houses facing into the court. If the hypothesis be true that in this community the formation of friendships depends upon the extent of passive contacts, the people living in these end houses will receive fewer sociometric choices from their court neighbors than will the people living in houses facing into the court.

Table 6 shows the number of choices given to people living in each house position for the six large courts. The letters in Row 1 symbolize each house position and correspond to the letters in Figure 5. The letters *a* and *m* stand for the end houses in each court. Row 2 is the total number of choices received by

Table 6.—The Number of Sociometric Choices Received from Their Court Neighbors by People Living in Each House Position in the Six Large Westgate Courts

1. House position	a	b	c	d	e	f	g	h	i	j	k	l	m
2. Total number of choices received (1)*	4	9	7	10	11	6	13	11	9	8	10	9	5
3. Mean number of choices received (.25)*	.67	1.50	1.17	1.67	1.83	1.00	2.17	1.83	1.50	1.33	1.67	1.50	.83

Mean number of choices received by all inner houses facing into the court ($b-l$) = 1.56
Mean number of choices received by all end houses facing the street (a and m) = 0.60
* Total and mean not including the end houses facing into their courts

people living in each house position from people living in their own court. The mean number of choices received by people in each position is presented in Row 3. The unbracketed figures in column *a* are the total and mean choices received by all six of the end houses in this position. It should be kept in mind, however, that only four of these six houses face out on the street, the other two facing into the court. The figures in brackets are the total and mean choices received by the four houses facing the street.

Examination of the figures in this table makes it clear that the people living in these end houses receive fewer choices than the people living in any other house position. The mean number of choices received by people living in end houses facing the street is 0.60 and by people living in inner court houses is 1.56. This difference is consistent throughout. In each of the six courts the inner court residents receive a larger mean number of choices than the residents in end houses facing the street.[4]

Let us now examine the effects of functional distance in Westgate West. Figure 3 shows that each building has a long porch on each floor with the entrances to each apartment opening out onto the porch. Short stairways lead up to each of the lower-floor apartments. Outside stairways at each end of the lower-floor porch connect the two floors, and form the only paths by which upper-floor people can reach their floor.

The left-hand stairway connecting the two floors passes directly in front of the doorway of apartment 1 and close to the door of apartment 7. The connecting stairway on the right passes close by, though not directly in front of, the doorway to apartment 5, and directly between the doorways of the two right-hand apartments, 9 and 10, on the upper floor.

Each of the lower-floor apartments has a small mailbox directly adjoining its doorway. Near the lower-floor apartment 5 is a

[4] Significant at the 3 per cent level of confidence.

cluster of five mailboxes which serve all of the upper-floor apartments.

These are the details of construction which of themselves will determine the required paths followed in moving in or out of the building. From the nature of these details of design and the required paths they impose on the residents of these buildings, it is possible to make a number of derivations about the relative frequency of passive contacts and, consequently, the sociometric choices exchanged among particular people or groups of people living in each of the buildings. These derivations demand only one assumption—that the people living in these barracks will most frequently use the shortest path between their apartment and their destination.

1. *The people living in the end apartments 1 and 5 on the lower floor should receive from and give to the upper-floor residents more sociometric choices than the people living in any other apartment on the lower floor.*

We can expect this because apartments 1 and 5 are at the foot of the stairways connecting the two floors and are, therefore, the only lower-floor apartments which upper-floor residents must pass in entering or leaving the building. In using the left-hand stairway, upper-floor people must pass directly in front of the doorway of apartment 1. In using the right-hand stairway, upper-floor people pass close to, though not directly in front of, the doorway of apartment 5. In going to their mailboxes upper-floor people do pass the doorway of apartment 5.

Table 7 presents the number of sociometric choices lower-floor people give to and receive from people living on the upper floor. The figures in Row 1 are the apartment numbers as diagrammed in Figure 3. Row 2 presents the number of choices the people in each apartment position on the lower floor give to people on the upper floor of their building, and row 3 presents the number of choices lower-floor people receive from their upstairs neighbors.

The figures in Rows 2 and 3 are the combined totals for all seventeen buildings.

We see, then, that the end apartments on the lower floor give far more choices to upper-floor people than do any of the other apartments. The end apartments average 12 choices each to upstairs neighbors, compared to only 6.33 for the three middle apartments. Choices given by apartments 1 and 5 are significantly higher than choices given by 2, 3, and 4 at the 5 per cent level of confidence.[5]

Table 7.—*The Number of Sociometric Choices the Lower-Floor People Give to and Receive from People Living on the Upper Floors of the Westgate West Buildings*

1. Apartment position	1	2	3	4	5
2. Choices given to upper floor	13	5	8	6	11
3. Choices received from upper floor	14	3	12	4	15

Similarly, the end apartments receive more choices from the upper floor than do any of their lower-floor neighbors. They receive an average of 14.5 choices each and the three middle apartments receive only an average of 6.33 choices apiece. Apartments 1 and 5 differ from apartments 2 and 4 at the 5 per cent level of significance. They do not, however, differ significantly from middle apartment 3.

Clearly the derivation is upheld. The end apartments on the lower floor both give and receive more upper-floor choices than do any of the other lower-floor apartments. A theoretical difficulty, however, exists in the unusually high number of choices which middle apartment 3 receives from the upper floor. Apartment 3 receives twelve choices, while its immediate neighbors,

[5] Significance of differences, unless otherwise noted, were calculated by means of an analysis of variance. The significance consequently depends upon the consistency of the results among all the separate buildings.

apartments 2 and 4, receive only three and four choices respectively. Even if, for some reason we know nothing about, upper-floor people should have to pass by apartment 3, they would also have to pass apartments 2 and 4 and passive contacts with upper-floor people should be about the same for all three apartments. We have not been able to find an unequivocal explanation for the large number of choices of apartment 3 by their upstairs neighbors. One possible explanation is that the people in apartment 3, as will be shown later, receive the greatest number of lower-floor choices, and perhaps could meet more upper-floor people through their many lower-floor friends. However, this possible factor seems hardly sufficient to account for the observed data and the high number of upper-floor choices received by apartment 3 remains the one puzzling inconsistency in the body of data.

Table 7 helps to explain the peculiar shape noted in the lower curve in Figure 4 which plots the choices exchanged between floors. This curve has about the same high level for distance units S and 1S, then a sudden drop to a low level at which distances 2S, 3S, and 4S all have about the same value. Distance units S and 1S are made up largely of choices exchanged between end apartments 1 and 5 and the upper floor, while distances 2S, 3S, and 4S are made up predominantly of choices exchanged between the upper floor and the middle apartments 2, 3, and 4. This explanation of the shape of this curve also suggests that for choices between floors, functional distance is far more important than physical distance.

In line with this explanation, we would expect that the end apartments on the first floor would give and receive a high number of upper-floor choices whereas the middle apartments, 2, 3, and 4, would give and receive a uniformly low number of upper-floor choices. Table 7 shows that this is true for choices given to the upper floor and, with the exception of apartment 3, also true for choices received from the upper floor.

2. *Apartments 1 and 6 should exchange more choices than apartments 2 and 7. Similarly, apartments 5 and 10 should exchange more choices than apartments 4 and 9.*

Apartments 1 and 6 and apartments 2 and 7 are both exactly 53 feet apart. However in using the left-hand stairway, the people in apartment 6 must pass by apartment 1, whereas the people living in 7 will not pass by apartment 2. Therefore we can expect that there will be many more passive contacts between 1 and 6 than between 2 and 7, and there should consequently be more choices between 1 and 6 than between 2 and 7. The data substantiate this derivation. Apartments 1 and 6 exchange eleven choices and apartments 2 and 7 only four choices.

The same considerations should apply for choices between 5 and 10 as compared with 4 and 9. These apartments are within seven feet of being equidistant. Apartments 5 and 10 exchange nine choices while 4 and 9 give each other four choices. The Chi Square test for both sets of differences combined is significant at almost the 1 per cent level.

These data give clear evidence that it is possible to have equal physical distances but very different functional distances.

3. *Apartment 7 will choose 6 more than it will choose 8; apartment 9 will choose 10 more than it will choose 8. This will not be true for first-floor apartments in similar positions.*

Apartments 6 and 7 will use predominantly the left-hand stairway. Apartments 9 and 10 will use predominantly the right-hand stairway. Apartment 8, however, which is approximately equidistant from both stairways should sometimes use one end and sometimes the other. Therefore, there should be a greater number of passive contacts between 6 and 7 and between 9 and 10 than between 7 and 8 or 9 and 8. Again the sociometric data bear out the derivation. The choices from apartment 7 to 6 and from apartment 9 to 10 add up to a total of nineteen. They give to apartment 8, however, a total of only ten choices. The Chi Square for this difference is significant at almost the 2 per cent level.

We should not expect this result on the first floor since each of the apartments has its own short stairway leading to the outside of the building. Apartment 2 gives to apartment 1, and 4 gives to 5, a total of twenty choices. Apartments 2 and 4 give seventeen choices to apartment 3. This difference is not significant.

4. *The upper-floor choices apartment 1 gives and receives should be concentrated in apartments 6 and 7 and should taper off for apartments 8, 9, and 10. The upper-floor choices apartment 5 gives and receives should still be heaviest for apartments 9 and 10 but should decrease more gradually for apartments 8, 7 and 6.*

Only apartments 6 and 7 use the left-hand stairway consistently; 8, located between the two stairways, uses it occasionally, and 9 and 10 only rarely if at all. Therefore, apartment 1 will make most contacts with 6 and 7, a few with 8, and almost none at all with 9 and 10. The data in Table 8 support this

Table 8.—Upper-Floor Choices Apartments 1 and 5 Give and Receive

Apartment position	6	7	8	9	10
Choices 1 gives	6	4	2	1	0
Choices 1 receives	5	5	2	1	1
Choices 5 gives	1	1	3	2	4
Choices 5 receives	2	1	4	3	5

derivation. Apartment 1 gives ten of its thirteen choices to 6 and 7, two choices to 8, one to 9, and none at all to 10. Of the fourteen choices 1 receives, ten come from apartments 6 and 7, two from 8, and one each from 9 and 10.

Numbers 9 and 10 are the only upstairs apartments that use the right-hand connecting stairway consistently in order to leave the building. Though this stairway does not pass directly in front of number 5, the people using it also use the short stairway out from the lower porch which is used by apartment 5 and are likely, therefore, to make contacts with 5. Apartment 8 will use the right-hand stairway occasionally in leaving the building, and 6 and 7 only rarely. In addition, however, upper-floor people who wish to go to their mailboxes will pass apartment 5. Therefore, apartment 5 will make contacts with all upper-floor persons, but the most frequent contacts will be made with 9 and 10. Again the data support the derivation. Table 8 shows that 9 and 10 receive six of the eleven choices apartment 5 makes, 8 receives three choices, and 7 and 6 one choice apiece. Similarly, aparments 9 and 10 give eight of the fifteen upstairs choices 5 receives, and the remaining seven are received from apartments 6, 7, and 8. As predicted, apartment 1 has a heavier concentration of choices in 6 and 7 than does apartment 5 in 9 and 10. Twenty of the twenty-seven choices apartment 1 gives and receives are concentrated in apartments 6 and 7, whereas only fourteen of the twenty-six choices made by and to apartment 5 are centered in apartments 9 and 10. For this difference Chi Square is significant at about the 12 per cent level.

The data so far presented all support the hypotheses from which the numerous derivations about the effects of physical and functional factors were made. These hypotheses stated simply that in these two communities friendships will depend upon the occurrence of passive contacts and that the pattern and frequency of passive contacts among particular people will depend upon the ecological factors of physical and functional distance. The only finding inconsistent with these hypotheses is the large number of choices which the lower-floor middle apartment receives from upper-floor residents. There are, however, implicit in these hypotheses a series of rather interesting derivations which it has been impossible to check because of the great difficulty of isolating the effects of physical and functional distance.

Let us assume that we have a row of five identically designed houses with equal physical distance between any two adjoining houses. For reference we may label these houses a, b, c, d, and e in order along the row.

It is apparent that of all five house positions, the middle house, c, has the minimum total separation from all other houses in the row. The farther a house is from the middle position, the greater is its total physical separation from all other houses in the row.

Let us assume that within any given time interval the probability of a passive contact occurring between residents of houses which are one unit apart is greater than the probability of a contact occurring between residents of houses 2 units apart and so on. The probability of a passive contact occurring between residents living 4 units apart would be lowest.

The resident of house c will generally have made contact with all others living in the row sooner than any other resident. If enough time is allowed to elapse one might be relatively certain that all residents would have had at least one passive contact with all others in the row, but the resident in house c will have had the greatest number of such contacts, the residents of houses b and d the next largest number, and the residents of houses a and e would have had the least number. Therefore, we can expect that if a sociometric test were administered c would receive the greatest number of choices, b and d somewhat fewer choices, and a and e fewest choices of all. Thus, if we plotted a curve of number of choices against house position, we would expect a symmetrical curve monotonically decreasing with distance from the central position. Further, we would expect that as more and more contacts are made among all people living in this row with the passage of time, the curve would tend to flatten out.

To check these derivations specifically against the data available for Westgate and Westgate West is impossible, because in all cases both physical and functional distance have influenced the assignment of sociometric choices. A specific case may illustrate the difficulties involved. The lower floors of the Westgate West buildings resemble the theoretical arrangement of houses suggested above. There are five apartments arranged in a row with roughly equal physical separations between all apartments. Functionally, however, the two end apartments are very different from the middle apartments, for they are at the foot of the stairways connecting the two floors and therefore make many passive contacts with upstairs people. This increased number of between-floor contacts affects the relation the people in the end apartments have with others on their own floor. Table 9 presents

Table 9.—Number of Sociometric Choices Given to Each Lower-Floor Apartment Position by People Living on the Lower Floor

Apartment position	1	2	3	4	5
Number of sociometric choices	22	19	28	11	17

the data on the number of choices given to each apartment position by people living on the lower floor. Indeed, there is a peak at the middle apartment. The number of choices received by apartment 3 is greater at the 5 per cent level of significance than the number received by the other lower-floor apartments. Contrary to expectations, apartment 1 receives more choices than 2, and 5 receives more choices than 4.

In analyzing the data specifically for choices exchanged between particular apartment positions, we learn that apartment 4 gives 5 a total of nine choices whereas 5 gives 4 only four choices. Similarly, 2 gives eleven choices to apartment 1 and receives nine choices from 1. Thus, the major part of the differences between 5 and 4, and 1 and 2, is made up of unreciprocated choices from 4 and 2 to 5 and 1. The fact that many of these choices go unreciprocated is explained by the functional relationships between the end apartments 1 and 5, and the upper floor. Since these end apartments make so many passive contacts with the upper-floor residents, many of their choices will inevitably go to upper-floor people (see Table 7). Since the sociometric question limited the number of choices to three, it necessarily follows that many of the lower-floor choices to the end apartments must go unreciprocated.

The Ecological Basis for Formation of Groups

The data presented have been stated largely in terms of specific friendships between people living in particular house positions. We have shown that, in these two communities, friendships will be determined in large part by physical and functional distance. In terms of these ecological considerations we can further expect that a large proportion of all sociometric choices will be exchanged among people living within the same court or building. We know that in a Westgate court the houses are close to one another and with a few exceptions face into the same area. In general, the people living in each court are both physically and functionally closer to one another than to anyone else living in Westgate. This is obviously also true for the people living in each Westgate West building. The data corroborate the expectation. Of the 426 choices made by Westgate West people, 278 or 65.3 per cent were given to people living in the same building as the choosers. Similarly for Westgate, 143 or 55.5 per cent of the 258 choices made were given to people living in the same court as the choosers. Further, 85.5 per cent of all people in Westgate West chose at least one person living in the same building and 80 per cent of Westgaters chose at least one person in their court. If the end houses facing the street, which positionally at least are not members of the court, are excluded from this count, the figure for Westgate rises to 87.4 per cent. Thus, a large share of all friendships in both of these communities was among people living in the same court or building.

If one accepts the definition of a group as a number of inter-acting and sociometrically connected people, it follows that these ecological factors determine not only specific friendships but the composition of groups within these communities as well. Each court and building is populated by people who have most of their friends in the same living unit. Thus the people in each court or building will work together, play together, and, in general, see more of each other than of any other individuals living in the projects.

SUMMARY

The hypothesis has been advanced that friendships and group membership will be determined in these communities by passive contacts between neighbors. The pattern and number of such contacts among particular people will depend upon physical and functional distance. Data have been presented which reveal a striking relationship between these ecological factors and socio-metric choice.

Obviously, there are other methods of making friends. The men of the project undoubtedly meet one another in class and school activities. People probably meet at parties, and so on. However, the relationships between ecological and sociometric structures is so very marked that there can be little doubt that in these communities passive contacts are a major determinant of friendship and group formation. Further, we know from the data presented in Chapter 2 that these friendships are very active relationships and compose the major portion of the social lives of these people.

It should be remembered that Westgate and Westgate West represent homogeneous communities. Whether these ecological factors would be as effective in more heterogeneous communities is, of course, a question for further empirical study. It seems likely that in such communities ecological factors will play some part, though a less important one, in determining sociometric structure.

4

The Growth of a Tenant
Organization

As THE preceding chapter showed, friendships and social ties in Westgate and Westgate West are determined to a great extent by ecological factors. More than 60 per cent of all sociometric choices are made inside the chooser's court or building. The Westgate court or Westgate West building consitutes the major social unit.

The major portion of the remainder of this volume is devoted to an analysis, in terms of group standards and communication, of the reactions of each of these discrete social units, the courts and buildings, to a tenants' organization.

The Westgate Council, organized by the tenants themselves, represents the attempt by the residents to organize the whole community into a single functioning unit. The avowed purposes of the Council were: (1) to constitute a central agency representing all of Westgate for liaison purposes with the outside world, (2) to organize internal affairs and business of the community itself—e.g., employment agency, cooperative buying, etc., and (3) to promote social life within the project.

The first community meeting to plan an organization of some kind was called in Westgate about nine months after the courts had been fully occupied. By the time Westgate West, occupied later, was admitted to the organization, the Council had been established and been conducting regular meetings for some

months. It was not, however, launched without encountering
many obstacles.

THE RECEPTIVITY OF WESTGATERS TO THE IDEA OF AN ORGANIZATION

The early months of Westgate's existence were, for its tenants,
a period of adaptation and orientation—getting settled, buying
furniture, learning where the stores were, and slowly meeting
neighbors and making friends. Six months after the project had
been occupied, and when community life had probably become
reasonably stable, the interviews described in Chapter 2 were
held. Several of the questions were concerned specifically with
community activities and the possibilities of organization. The
answers show the general climate of opinion and receptivity to
the idea of a community organization that preceded the first
attempts to start such an organization.

In reply to the question, "What community activities should
there be in Westgate?" these responses were elicited:

No need for community activities		30%
Want some kind of community-wide organization		8%
Proposals for specific kinds of activities		62%
Special interest clubs°	35%	
Social activities (dances, picnics, etc.)	20%	
Activities for the children	18%	

° Percentages add up to more than 62, for some respondents made
several suggestions.

Thirty per cent of respondents were either negative or pessi-
mistic about the possibilities, because "everyone is so busy" and
"it's always so difficult to start that kind of thing." On the other
hand, 62 per cent of all respondents made specific proposals.
They would like bridge clubs or community dances or mothers'
clubs or ball teams. Only 8 per cent spontaneously mentioned
the need for a community-wide organization and these few were
quite vague as to the purposes of such an organization. It seems

evident that at this time a fairly large section of Westgate showed more interest in specific social activities than in a community-wide organization.

This sort of evidence is, of course, fragmentary, but it does provide some indication of the predisposition to the idea of a tenants' organization. It seems safe to infer that at the time of this interview, four months before the first organizational meeting, only a handful of people were concerned with the notion of a tenants' organization. These few had only the vaguest ideas of how it should be organized and what purposes it should serve.

THE FORMATION OF THE COUNCIL

Suddenly something happened to create a spurt of interest. Late in the afternoon of a brisk, windy November day, a small, unexplained fire in a nearly completed Westgate West building was fanned into a roaring blaze. Westgaters were terrified. Their own homes, some less than fifty feet away from the burning building, were wooden frame structures with fiberboard walls. Men rushed home from their classes, climbed to the roofs of their own small houses, and with buckets, pans, and pots of water doused any stray sparks. Their efforts were successful, the blaze didn't spread; but the burning building was quickly reduced to a charred, uninhabitable shell.

Westgate came alive that evening. Petitions were circulated throughout the project requesting M.I.T. to provide fire alarm boxes inside the project. Volunteers canvassed the project raising money for the purchase of a fire hose. Everyone signed the petition and contributed to the hose fund.

This was the immediate stimulus to the founding of the organization. The few Westgaters who had thought seriously about the possibilities of organization got together, made plans, and some days after the fire prepared and distributed a leaflet calling a meeting.

The meeting developed into a somewhat ineffectual discussion, top-heavy with parliamentary procedure. About fifty of the 200 people in Westgate attended. The three founders, Robert A., Sidney L., and Milton L., had come prepared with a plan for organization and, armed with a superior knowledge of the "Rules of Order," quickly took control of the meeting. Before it was clear what was going on, Robert A. had nominated Sidney L. as temporary chairman, Milton L. seconded the nomination, the nominations closed, the matter was put to a vote, and Sidney L. was appointed chairman pro tem. The three founders then presented their plan for a central council made up of representatives from each of the nine courts. The plan and the general conduct of the meeting met with considerable resistance and the meeting ended in fruitless bickering.

A week later a second meeting was called. This meeting was somewhat improved in tone. Discussions of the form of organization continued, and a committee of ten people, including Robert A., Sidney L., and Milton L., was appointed to draw up a constitution.

These two meetings and the manner in which they were conducted were important in determining later attitudes toward the organization. Westgaters, who only a few months before thought of community activities in terms of bridge clubs and ball teams, suddenly found themselves caught in a welter of parliamentary procedure planning for a formal organization to represent and transact the business of the community. The resentment aroused in a goodly portion of the population is typified by this statement:

I went to one meeting. I didn't like the way it was run. They crammed the whole thing through in one hour; it was too formal in procedure. I'd have been more interested in an open meeting. A clique wanted their own plan and railroaded it through using all kinds of parliamentary procedure.

Some people, however, supported the founders and the plan they proposed strongly:

I was surprised at the meeting to see how little people know about government. They didn't see that 200 people was too large a group. People are cynical and think that representatives would be getting something out of it. Some people don't like a thing if they don't have the idea themselves. Some people think that it's sort of a political job. They think it elevates people to be representatives. They don't see it's just lots of work—it's an unpaid job.

THE CONSTITUTION

The Committee on Organization labored and in a few weeks produced a constitution setting up an organization with these main features:

1. A central council shall be the nucleus of the organization.
2. The council shall be composed of two representatives chosen by popular vote from each court.
3. Open meetings shall be held at least twice monthly.

The constitution and a ballot were submitted to all residents of Westgate and it was approved by a vote of 167 to 7.

The committee interpreted the vote as an indication of over-whelming approval and support and proceeded to set up a functioning organization. Data from our informal interviews, however, suggest that perhaps half of those who voted approval had not a very active interest in the organization.

THE FUNCTIONING OF THE WESTGATE COUNCIL

In January most of the courts elected representatives and these delegates met briefly to elect a chairman and a clerk. The regular business meetings began at the beginning of the spring term late in February.

To implement the functioning of the Council, a number of innovations were introduced in the early meetings: (1) a treasurer was appointed, (2) a number of specialized committees (e.g. social liaison, economic, etc.) were started, each with its own chairman and volunteer membership, (3) the delegates from each court were asked to hold regular meetings with their court members to discuss with them the progress of the Council and to get suggestions for possible projects or improvements.

The meetings of the Council were held twice monthly. The subject of the meetings centered almost exclusively around a series of projects for the general improvement of life in Westgate. Twenty projects were started. Of these, four were dropped, eight completed, and the remainder were puttering along half-heartedly at the time we discontinued our formal observations at the end of May.[1] The four projects dropped were the most ambitious and important activities of the lot—a nursery school, a co-op grocery, a community laundry, and a community recreation building. Plans that were carried out included an Easter egg roll, a splash party in the M.I.T. swimming pool, a Westgate directory, an exercise class for women, a price reduction from the cleaner, an employment bureau for Westgate wives, a story on the Westgate Council in the M.I.T. newspaper, *The Tech*, and a block party for everyone in Westgate and Westgate West.

It rained the day of the egg roll and the eggs had to be returned; only ten of the 270 couples in the two projects showed up for the splash party; *The Tech* cut down the long story the liaison committee had prepared to a few paragraphs on a back page; only about a third of the tenants took advantage of the cleaning reduction and only a handful of people asked for any help from the employment bureau. In short, in its four months of existence, the Westgate Council had succeeded in three things—

[1] After the completion of our study, many important projects which had been dropped or were still pending were made possible by a grant of money and equipment from the Massachusetts Institute of Technology and The Technology Christian Association. The data presented show the picture during the period of our study.

a directory of Westgate, a moderately well attended exercise class, and a block party.

Attendance at the Council meetings also serves as an indicator of the effectiveness of the Council in keeping its membership interested and involved. Though the meetings were open, attendance consisted usually of just the officials, court delegates, and committee members of the organization. Howe Court had been so little interested in the organization that it neglected even to elect a representative. Main Court, while hostile to the organization, had one self-appointed representative, who showed up sporadically only because he was a close friend of the chairman. Freeman and Williams Courts, while not markedly unfriendly, were somewhat apathetic and attendance from these courts, too, was rather irregular.

In summary, by late May, when our standardized interviews were undertaken, the Westgate Council had been in existence four months. Its record of accomplishments during this period had been notably barren and toward the end of the term even the interest of many court delegates had begun to wane.

ATTITUDES TOWARD THE ORGANIZATION

As a result of the combination of organizational difficulties and confusions about the purposes of the organization, many people had been reluctant to cooperate with or participate in the activities of the Council. Essentially the active element in the organization consisted of some twenty-five people and their spouses, most of whom did double duty as Council officials, court delegates, and volunteer committee members. The remainder of the population were either openly hostile or passively in favor of the organization and the Council seemed unable to enlist the active support of any but this small nucleus.

Specific explanations of the "reasons" for attitudes such as these are extremely complex and beyond the scope of this study.

However, our observations lead to some hunches about their main determinants.

1. The interviews held before the inception of the Council indicated that a considerable section of the population was genuinely opposed or indifferent to formal organization of any kind. Almost all of the people who did manifest any interest in community activities favored social activities of one kind or another. Most of the people simply were not interested in organized activities. Their attitudes ranged from the mild but definite statement of a housewife, "There's nothing wrong with organizations but I've never been the kind who could get involved in them," to the embittered protest of a veteran, "I had enough of that kind of thing in the army. If there's anything formal or organized about it, I don't want to have anything to do with it."

2. The preliminary organizational meetings had created an extremely bad first impression. They had been conducted in so formal and high-handed a manner that six months afterwards the impression was still widespread that "someone's trying to become a big shot out of this thing."

3. The Council's almost continuous record of failure served to reinforce and confirm the attitudes of those initially hostile and to discourage those people who were favorable and active in the work of the Council.

Yet the fact remains that despite the discouraging history of the Council, about one-fourth of the population were favorable and active in Council affairs and about one-fourth were also favorably inclined, although they took no active part in the affairs of the organization. Explanations of these favorable attitudes are somewhat less clear. Interview statements from these people are constistently somewhat vague—"I'm all for it, it can do a lot of good."

This much, however, seems clear:

1. In general, the people who were favorable to the organiza-

tion had a considerably wider range of experience with organizations than did those who were unfavorable. And, of course, these favorable people were much less resistant to the "idea" of formal organization.

2. Most of the people who were favorable and active had been involved in one way or another in the formation of the organization and had a considerable stake in its success.

3. Most of the people who were favorable had close friendship ties with one another and were members of the same face-to-face groups. The importance of friendships and group membership in spreading and perpetuating attitudes of this kind cannot be overemphasized and the next two chapters will be devoted to a detailed examination of the effects of these factors on attitudes, both favorable and unfavorable.

WESTGATE WEST AND THE COUNCIL

Westgate West was fully occupied by February of 1947, the same month that the Council began its first formal meetings. From the first, the subject of Westgate West's relationship to the Council had been a recurrent item on the agenda. The issue was never whether or not Westgate West should become a part of the tenants' organization but rather how and in what form the invitation to join should be extended. After some preliminary debate the following letter was distributed:

TO THE RESIDENTS OF WESTGATE WEST:

Are you interested in an organization to promote the social, economic, and general welfare of your community? The residents of Westgate invite you to join their newly formed organization!!

FOR WHAT PURPOSE?

Mainly to get better acquainted among ourselves, to set up committees to handle employment for wives (including baby-sitting problems etc.), to act as a unit when making recommendations to M.I.T., and to sponsor social events, sports events, etc.

Our Council consists of two representatives from each court headed by a chairman and clerk. Individual court meetings are held prior to each Council meeting, giving the councilmen a representative viewpoint in making decisions for the whole.

If you are interested please come to our next Council meeting to be held in Room 5-112 at 7:30 P.M. Wednesday, March 26, 1947.

Sincerely yours,
WESTGATE COUNCIL

Eighteen people from Westgate West attended this March 26th meeting and the evening was devoted largely to a discussion of the problem of the form of representation for Westgate West in the Council. A committee was appointed to draw up a plan for representation. This committee, made up of people from both Westgate and Westgate West, formulated a plan according to which each of the 17 buildings would have one representative in the Council. This plan was overwhelmingly approved. Most of the buildings quickly elected representatives, and on April 23 representatives from the two projects met together officially for the first time.

A striking contrast in attitude between the two projects quickly became apparent. Westgate West displayed a marked enthusiasm for the organization. This difference shows up in the records of attendance at the Council meetings. Figure 7 reveals that for the last three meetings of the spring term, after Westgate West had been officially admitted to the Council, the interest of the Westgate delegates had definitely begun to lag. Less than half of the elected Westgate delegates attended these three meetings, while Westgate West delegates turned out in almost full force for them.

In addition, the responsiveness of the two groups to the Council's projects was quite different. For example, the economics committee had induced a cleaning establishment to give the residents of the two projects a 15 per cent reduction in the price of dry cleaning. About 90 per cent of those who took advantage of this reduction were residents of Westgate West.

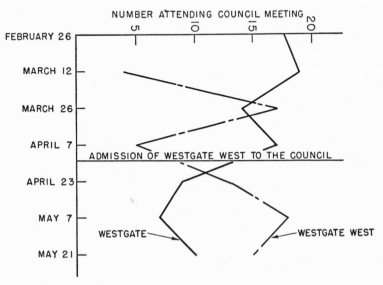

Fig. 7.   Attendance at Meetings of the Westgate Council

Though not fully documented, the explanation for this striking difference seems reasonably clear.

1. Almost everyone living in Westgate during the spring term had been around at the birth of the organization and subjected to the unpleasantness of the first meetings; for Westgate West the organization represented a going concern.

2. By the time of the November organizational meetings, Westgate had been in existence nine months and had become a reasonably settled community with fairly stable social groupings.

When Westgate West was admitted to the Council it, on the other hand, had been fully occupied only two and a half months. It seems likely, therefore, that the organization satisfied certain social needs for Westgate West which no longer existed in Westgate. At one meeting a newly elected Westgate West delegate testified that the first time he had met everyone living in his building was at the meeting to elect a building representative.

3. At the time it joined the council Westgate West was physically still in a somewhat primitive condition. Sidewalks hadn't been laid, no landscaping had been undertaken, few telephones were available, house numbers had not been posted, etc. The possible advantages of collective action were, therefore, far more obvious than in Westgate which was a finished community.

5

The Operation of Group Standards

THE TERM "group standard" or "group norm" has been used freely either to describe or to explain the rather well substantiated finding that members of the same face-to-face group exhibit relative uniformity with respect to specified opinions and modes of behavior. The use of the term, whether in a descriptive or an explanatory manner, has generally carried with it the meaning that this observed uniformity derives in some manner from influences which the group is able to exert over its members. The fact that members of some social set all have relatively similar tastes in, for example, selecting recreational activities, has generally been explained on the basis of inter-individual or group influences rather than on the basis of similar circumstances producing similar but independent reactions in a number of people.

There is no question any longer that individuals and groups do exert influences on others which can and do result in uniform opinions and behavior patterns. There have been many studies which have demonstrated the existence and importance of this phenomenon. The classic experiment by Sheriff[1] clearly demonstrated that, at least in a situation which was almost completely unstructured, the individual was virtually entirely dependent upon the group for forming a stable mode of response. The strength of the group influence was plainly sufficient to override most individual factors.

[1] Sheriff, M., *The Psychology of Social Norms*. New York: Harper & Brothers, 1936.

It has also been shown, by a series of independent studies,[2] that people's aspirations and goal-setting behavior are strongly influenced by information they possess about how others behave and their relationship to these others. All of these influences produce changes in the individual's behavior which result in his being more similar to other members of the group to which he feels he belongs.

Once we depart from the well-controlled laboratory situation it is no longer easy to claim unequivocally that observed uniformity is due to group influence. Newcomb,[3] for example, in his study of a college community which had a reputation for being liberal found that students consistently became more liberal with increasing length of attendance at the college. It is possible plausibly to maintain that these changing attitudes resulted from group pressures and influences once the student became a member of the community. It would also, however, be possible to maintain that these changes occurred in different people independently as a result of the similar experiences, curricular and otherwise, to which they were all subjected in the rather unique college. The demonstration that a group standard existed would indeed be difficult. Such demonstration would have to rest upon a series of empirical facts concerning the means by which the group enforces the standard, the relation between the pattern of conformity and the group structure, and the relationship to the group of members who deviate from the standard.

The Westgate and Westgate West housing projects offered a unique opportunity for the study of group standards. We have shown that the court, in Westgate, and the building, in Westgate West, became the unit of social life. Friendship groups formed mainly within the court and within the building. The back-

[2] Lewin, *et. al.*, *"Level of Aspiration"* [in] *Personality and the Behavior Disorders.* Vol. I, pp. 333-78. New York: Ronald Press Co., 1944.

[3] Newcomb, T., *Personality and Social Change.* New York: Dryden Press, 1943.

grounds and interests of the residents were relatively homogeneous throughout both projects and the assignment of houses or
apartments to particular people had not been made on any kind
of selective basis. It was also clear that there had been no differential treatment of courts or of buildings. The study of group
standards might consequently be pursued fruitfully by carefully
examining the reasons for differences in behavior among these
social units where such differences emerged.

It was found that differences between courts did exist to a
rather marked extent on matters concerning the Westgate tenants'
organization. This organization was, at least potentially, of equal
relevance and importance to all residents of Westgate and of
Westgate West and all residents were urged to support it. Representation in the Westgate Council was on the basis of courts and
buildings and consequently called for action from each court and
each building. Yet, in spite of this equality of relevance, some
courts and buildings supported the organization, others were
overtly hostile, while still others were indifferent. We shall proceed to examine the determinants of these differences among
courts and among buildings to see whether group standards were
or were not operating and, if they were, how they made themselves effective.

ATTITUDES TOWARD THE WESTGATE COUNCIL

By May of 1947, when interview data concerning the attitudes
of residents toward the Westgate organization were collected,
the Council had almost completed the first semester of active
existence. Attitudes toward the new venture had had opportunity
to crystallize, and most tenants had decided whether or not they
cared to participate in its activities. Since the turnover in residents occurred mainly at the break between semesters, practically
all residents who were living there at the time of the interview

had been living in the project when the Council started its active program.

All of the 100 Westgate families and 166 of the 170 Westgate West families were asked, as part of a larger interview (see Appendix), "We understand there is a tenants organization here. What do you think of it? Are you active in it?" The interviewers were instructed to follow these questions with nondirective probes until they were satisfied that they had obtained an adequate picture of the attitude toward the organization and the degree and kind of participation in its activities. These data were then categorized in the following way:

Attitudes Toward the Organization

Favorable: People who considered the organization primarily a good thing. Usually they endorsed both the idea of organization as such and some aims of the Council. Statements ranged from warm approval, "I am definitely in favor of it. It's a worthwhile project. It's functioning well," to a vaguely approving, "It's all right."

Neutral: People who mentioned specific good and bad points about the organization so that no definitely favorable or unfavorable attitude could be assigned. In effect, this category included borderline people who had some basic attitude, but saw many points contrary to it. Examples are: "I guess it's all right if they accomplish something—I don't think they have as yet." "It's a good idea, but there are not too many problems for the community to deal with."

Apathetic: People who said they had not been interested enough to find out anything about the organization. In a sense this is a mildly unfavorable attitude—the organization did not concern them. On the other hand, they did not express any directly unfavorable opinion: "Don't know anything about it. Haven't been to any of the meetings or anything. Not knowing—I wouldn't want to say anything."

Unfavorable: People who expressed a definitely unfavorable opinion about the organization, that it was a waste of time, that the people in it were objectionable, that they never would achieve anything.

"A large majority of the members are reactionary. They give no attention to wider aspects." "It's unnecessary and high-schoolish."

Activities in the Organization

Active leader: People who took a definite part in the activities of the Council as a whole, as representatives, committee members, or doing volunteer work. "We've been to meetings as delegates two or three times. I volunteered as bartender for the block party." "I am one of the court representatives. I'm a member of the welcoming committee greeting new residents."

Active follower: People who, though not active in the sense of the previous category, had attended more than one court meeting. They cooperated with the Council as it was set up on the court level. They went to the meetings in which the representatives were elected. They listened to the representatives' reports of the Council's actions and gave their suggestions and complaints to be taken up in the next meeting. They were, therefore, a necessary working part of the organization although they took no part in the workings of the Council as such. "We have been to the building meetings, that's as far as it goes." "We go to the meetings, everybody goes to them."

Inactive: People who did not make any effort to keep in contact with the organization. This included both the people who belonged (that is, they considered themselves represented by the Council) and those who did not feel even a formal connection with the Council. From the point of view of actual behavior, these two groups are indistinguishable. "To be truthful, I'm not active. Splendid idea—but I'm too busy." The principal answer from this group was a curt "No." These people did not even attend court meetings.

The questions about attitudes and activity measure two different aspects of a person's relation to the organization. His attitude may stem from a variety of interests and beliefs. He may view the Council as a way of having certain needs satisfied, as a way to meet his fellow tenants, as unrelated to his needs, or as a childish pastime. It is clear that some of these ways of looking at the Council will lead more readily to activity than others. But a resident's actual activity will also depend on other factors—

whether he has time, whether a neighbor draws him into some work, whether he sees something that he personally can do. It is therefore possible that attitude and activity may occur together in all combinations although some are more likely than others. They are distinct, though correlated variables. Some examples will show how different attitudes and activities were combined in individual cases.

Jack and Marie L. had moved into Westgate only a few weeks before the first preparatory meeting of the organization. One of the founders of the Council lived in the same court and Marie attended all preliminary meetings. In an informal interview just before the adoption of the Council's constitution she underlined the necessity for adequate representation in the Council and she resented the aspersions of some people that the Council would just serve to give the "politicians a big play." She felt that this attempt at group action was a valuable experience in the one-sided training for engineers. She was also enthusiastic about the projects the Council could undertake, "everything the members want, laundry, financial aid, nursery school, a cooperative store, etc." In the first term of the Council's existence Mrs. L. was elected clerk of the Council, while Jack became chairman of a committee. Here we have a favorable attitude which led to active participation.

Two houses from the L.'s lived the T.'s. Ann T. had been interviewed in July, 1946. She had been skeptical about the chances of a tenants' organization. "I don't know whether it could accomplish anything. If John were in on it, maybe something could be done." The T.'s took little part in the formation of the Council. At the meeting where the committees were being formed Marie L. brought a few friends from her court with her, among them John T. When the composition of the social committee was being discussed Mrs. L. suggested John. It turned out that he was the only prospective member of the social committee present, and so he was asked to accept the chairmanship. He fulfilled his duties conscientiously, but in May, 1947, he told an interviewer, "I don't think there is any need for such an organization. The things we have done are trivial. I am head of one of the committees, so I shouldn't say so, but I think it is mainly a chance for the politically inclined to let off steam. Our committee has done one of the very few worthwhile things that have been done." Here an unfavorable attitude is overcome by a constellation of circumstances which made Mr. T. take an active part in the organization.

Dick and Winnie S. had moved into Westgate at the beginning of the spring term of 1947. He was a graduate student preparing for his general exams and working on a part-time appointment at M.I.T. Winnie was kept busy with a vivacious three-year-old daughter. A friend with a child of the same age who lived in a nearby apartment house often came over to have the child play in the yard. She formed few friendships within the project. Her opinion of the organization was rather favorable, but she felt that she had no time to participate. "Perhaps when Dick is finished with his exams. . . ." Here a favorable attitude does not lead to activity because of lack of opportunity and lack of social contacts which could have interested them in active work.

Frank and Helen J. had been among the earliest residents of Westgate. They found the small group in their court particularly congenial and they expressed no desire for other contacts. When they saw the first leaflets of the Council they considered them a curious idea, but did not attend the meetings. When the Council got under way Frank expressed this attitude, "I can't tell how these people are going to represent me. If I have any complaints I would rather see about it myself." None of their friends participated in the organization—the only resident of the court who attended Council meetings apologized that he went only to see that nothing was put over on them. Later in the spring Frank J.

had some conflict with the Council because his garden did not conform to the regulations which M.I.T. had set up and had asked the Council to enforce. Interviewed on his feelings about the Council he replied, "The only people who care are those who go around interviewing about it." Here, aided by the support of the court, an unfavorable attitude resulted in no participation.

PATTERNS OF ATTITUDE AND ACTIVITY

The observation that there are great differences from one court to another in attitude toward and activity in the tenants' organization implies that within any one court there is relative homogeneity with respect to both of these factors. In the extreme case where all members of a court coincided exactly on both of these dimensions the demonstration of homogeneity would be a simple matter. This extreme case does not, of course, occur and some method must be devised for describing the pattern within any court both with respect to the content of the pattern and the degree of homogeneity. That is, is it a favorable and active court or is it an unfavorable and inactive court; do 80 per cent of the court members show this behavior and attitude combination or do only 60 per cent of the court members show it?

It seemed feasible, from the nature of the data, to distinguish four possible types of court patterns, namely, favorable-active, favorable-inactive, unfavorable-active, and unfavorable-inactive. Once it was determined in which of these categories a court was located, the number of people in the court who conformed to or deviated from the court pattern could then be easily computed. When this was done it would be possible to proceed to a careful examination of whether or not the observed degree of homogeneity within courts was worthy of note and whether or not it could be attributed to the existence of group standards.

If only these four types of patterns are to be distinguished we must, for this purpose, do some additional combining of the original categories into which the data were classified. This presents no problem for the activity dimension. Clearly the active leader and active follower categories should both be called active. The combination of the attitude categories presents somewhat more of a problem, however. The extreme categories, favorable and unfavorable, clearly fall into their proper place. The categories of apathetic and neutral, however, are not quite so clear. It was reasoned that the apathetic people were at least mildly unfavorable to the organization since they either did not care to know about it or else had simply remained sufficiently out of things not to have heard about what was going on. On the basis of this reasoning the apathetic people were classed as unfavorable.

The few residents who were classified as neutral were really borderline cases. To some extent they were favorable and to some extent unfavorable. Whatever the court pattern happens to be they, in this sense, both conform and deviate from it on the attitude dimension. In accordance with this view, the neutral people were not considered in determining the court pattern. In any event there were too few people thus categorized to have affected this determination much. Once the court pattern was determined, these neutrals were regarded as conformers if they fell into the proper activity category and were, of course, considered deviates if they did not.

We shall describe the method used for determining the court pattern by means of an example shown in Table 10a. This table shows the attitude-activity distribution of Tolman Court. Looking first at the activity dimension we find that twelve residents were active and only one was not; on the attitude dimension nine residents were favorable and two were unfavorable. The classification of this court, then, is "favorable-active." In this case, following our procedure for neutrals, we shall consider anybody who was neutral and active as conforming to the group standard.

Of the two neutrals in the court, one followed the group standard
and the other did not. The conformers include everybody in the
quadrant favorable or neutral and active (leader or follower).
There were ten conformers and three deviates from the pattern.

Table 10.—*Examples of Court Patterns*

	Active leader	Active follower	Inactive	Total
a. FAVORABLE-ACTIVE (TOLMAN COURT)				
Favorable	5	4		9
Neutral		1	1	2
Unfavorable	1	1		2
TOTAL	6	6	1	13
b. UNFAVORABLE-INACTIVE (MAIN COURT)				
Favorable			1	1
Neutral	1			1
Apathetic			1	1
Unfavorable			4	4
TOTAL	1		6	7
c. FAVORABLE-INACTIVE (WILLIAMS COURT)				
Favorable	3		4	7
Neutral			3	3
Apathetic			2	2
Unfavorable			1	1
TOTAL	3		10	13

A different type of pattern is shown in Main Court (Table
10b). Here six of the seven residents were inactive, while five
were either apathetic or unfavorable. The pattern is therefore
"unfavorable-inactive." As the only neutral resident was active,
he cannot be considered as conforming to the pattern; he and
the favorable inactive resident were deviates; the five inactive
residents, who were either apathetic or unfavorable, conformed
to the pattern.

As a final example let us take a favorable-inactive pattern (Table 10c). In Williams Court, ten residents out of thirteen were inactive. Seven were favorable, while only three were apathetic or unfavorable. This pattern is therefore "favorable-inactive," and the three neutral-inactives conformed to the pattern. Here there is relatively little concentration in the quadrant corresponding to the pattern; seven residents conformed to it, and six were deviates.

Table 11.—Court Patterns in Westgate

Court	N	Favorable	Unfavorable	Active	Inactive	Number of Deviates
		a. FAVORABLE-ACTIVE				
Richards	7	5		7		2
Tolman	13	11		12		3
Freeman	13	9		8		5
Miller	13	12		8		6
Rotch	8	7		6		2
		b. FAVORABLE-INACTIVE				
Williams	13	10			10	6
		c. UNFAVORABLE-INACTIVE				
Carson	13		7		9	7
Howe	13		9*		7	3
Main	7		5		6	2

* One uncategorized.

This procedure was carried out for each of the nine Westgate courts and for each of the seventeen Westgate West buildings. The results are shown in Tables 11 and 12. In Westgate five of the courts showed a favorable-active pattern, one court showed a favorable-inactive pattern, and three courts showed an un-

favorable-inactive pattern. Wide differences did exist among the
courts. Also, within each court there was relative homogeneity.
Five of the nine courts had a small proportion of deviates. In all
but one of the courts the majority conformed to the court pattern.

Table 12.—Patterns in Westgate West

Buildings	N	Favorable neutral	Active	Inactive	Number of deviates
		a. FAVORABLE-ACTIVE			
201-10	9	8*	8		1
211-20	10	8*	10		1
221-30	10	10	9		1
231-40	10	10	8		2
241-50	10	10	8		2
251-60	10	8	8		2
261-70	8	6	8		2
271-80	10	8	7		3
281-90	10	10	8		2
291-300	10	9	6		5
301-310	10	7	6		5
311-320	10	9*	8		2
361-370	10	8	6		4
		b. FAVORABLE-INACTIVE			
321-30	9	6		8*	3
331-40	10	7		6	7
341-50	10	7		10	3
351-60	10	7		10	3

* One uncategorized.

In Westgate West the degree of homogeneity within the building
was perhaps even more striking. Only four of the seventeen
buildings had as many as 40 per cent deviates from the building
pattern and nine of the buildings had only one or two such
deviates. In contrast to Westgate, however, there were no marked

differences among the patterns of different buildings. Thirteen of the buildings had favorable-active patterns and four of them had favorable-inactive patterns. There were no buildings with an unfavorable pattern. While in Westgate there was evidence for homogeneity within the court and heterogeneity among the

Table 13.—Attitude-Activity Distributions (Percentage)

	Active leaders	Active followers	Inactive	Unclassified	Total
		a. WESTGATE			
		(N=100)			
Favorable	22	14	18		54
Neutral	2	6	4		12
Apathetic		1	15		16
Unfavorable	2	2	13		17
Unclassified			1		1
TOTAL	26	23	51		100
		b. WESTGATE WEST			
		(N=166)			
Favorable	16	38	24	1	79
Neutral		2	1		3
Apathetic	1	2	8		11
Unfavorable	1		3		4
Unclassified		2	1		3
TOTAL	18	44	37	1	100

Significance of difference between Westgate and Westgate West:
Attitude $x^2=37.86$; $p=.01$
Activity $x^2=12.42$; $p=.01$

courts, in Westgate West there seems to have been the same amount of homogeneity among buildings as was found within the building.

If we combine all courts into an over-all Westgate pattern and all buildings into an over-all Westgate West pattern, this difference between the two projects emerges even more clearly. These over-all patterns for the two projects are shown in Table 13. In Westgate no homogeneous over-all pattern exists. Fifty-four per cent of the residents were favorable and 33 per cent were unfavorable or apathetic. Forty-nine per cent were active and 51 per cent were inactive. If we use the same criteria for determining the over-all pattern here as was used for the individual courts, we would conclude that Westgate had a favorable-inactive pattern from which 78 per cent of the residents deviated. Clearly the greatest concentrations were in the favorable-active and the unfavorable-inactive quadrants. Even if we depart from our rigorous method of determining patterns and regard the pattern in Westgate as favorable-active we still find that a majority (56 per cent) of the residents were deviates.

The situation in Westgate West is clearly different. Here 79 per cent of the residents were favorable and only 15 per cent were unfavorable or apathetic. Sixty-two per cent of the residents were active and 37 per cent were inactive. The over-all pattern is favorable-active. Most of the deviation that did occur from this pattern was on the activity dimension with little deviation on the attitude dimension.

What may we conclude from this analysis of the patterns within Westgate and within Westgate West? Do we as yet have any evidence for asserting the existence or nonexistence of group standards? With regard to Westgate we can clearly say that there was no group standard for the project as a whole. There were obviously opposing subgroups within Westgate with regard to both attitude and activity. Can one, however, maintain that there were group standards within each court? At this point this conclusion would seem plausible although it is by no means unequivocally demonstrated. We must, however, find some explanation why different courts, each composed of the same kinds of people in the same kinds of circumstances, reacted so differently from each other toward the organization and why, in spite of different reactions from different courts, there was relatively homogeneous behavior within each court. We at least are led to suspect that group standards or group norms were operating. In Westgate West, however, we cannot come to the same conclusions. Here it is possible that a group standard existed for the project as a whole, it is possible that group standards existed within each building, and it is possible that no group standards or norms existed at all but that the obtained high degree of uniformity was due to similar independent reactions of the residents to the same state of affairs. As we have pointed out before, the hypothesis that the uniformity in Westgate West resulted from similar independent reactions of the residents seems probable on the basis of several considerations. Unlike the residents of Westgate, who had been living there up to fifteen months and had had four months' actual experience with the organization, the residents of Westgate West were all relative newcomers. The oldest residents of Westgate West had only been living there about five months and their contact with the Westgate organization had been limited. It was only about one month prior to the collection of these data that Westgate West actually joined the organization. We might expect, then, that in Westgate West, where the social groupings had not had time to form into cohesive units and where the contact with the tenants' organization was only recent, group norms would not have developed to any considerable degree. The tenants, however, all in the same situation and pretty much the same kinds of people, tended, individually, to react favorably to the organization.

THE EVIDENCE FOR GROUP STANDARDS

On the basis of an examination of the actual distribution of conformity to and deviation from patterns of majority behavior, we have arrived at hypotheses concerning the reasons behind the observed degree of uniformity. It has seemed reasonable to suppose that group standards existed in the Westgate courts but that none existed in Westgate West. If this is true there should be other differences between these two projects which would support these hypotheses. One derivation may immediately be made. If the behavior in Westgate was determined largely by group influences while the behavior in Westgate West was determined largely by individual reactions, then individual differences on relevant factors should show more relationship to attitude and activity in Westgate West than in Westgate.

The personal reasons which residents of the two projects gave for their attitudes and for whether or not they participated in the activities of the organization were numerous and varied. Some people had special interests which were aided by the organization; some did not believe in organized activities in general; some said they had no time; some felt that their efforts would be fruitless for the short time that remained for them to stay in the project. All these factors, and others of the same kind, were influences acting on the individual, independently of the group to which he belonged. It would have been desirable, but almost impossible, to obtain reliable indications as to whether or not each of these factors was operating on a particular individual. Reliable data are at hand, however, concerning the length of time they expected to remain in the project. This, of course, coincided with the length of time they expected to remain in school and was fairly frequently mentioned as a reason for not participating in the activities of the tenants' organization.

The relationships between the expected length of further stay in the project and attitudes toward and acivity in the tenants organization are shown in Tables 14 and 15 for Westgate and Westgate West respectively. The time intervals used in these tables correspond to the college semesters. The first group, 0 to 1 month, was planning to leave the project at the end of the current semester, a few weeks after the interview took place. The last group, fourteen or more months, was going to stay at least until the end of the following academic year. Due to some of the uncertainties of college life many students in this last group could not give a very exact estimate of their expected length of stay.

Table 14.—Relation Between Expected Length of Stay and Attitude-Activity For Westgate

a. ATTITUDE*

Expected stay (months)	Favorable	Neutral apathetic	Unfavorable
0– 1	9	5	2
2– 5	12	6	4
6–13	16	11	5
14 plus	17	6	6
MEDIAN (months)	12	9	13

b. ACTIVITY

	Active leaders	Active followers	Inactive
0– 1	3	6	7
2– 5	6	4	12
6–13	7	9	17
14 plus	10	4	15
MEDIAN (months)	12	9	12

X^2 not significant for both sections of table.

* One uncategorized.

Consequently, the median expected length of residence was computed rather than the mean. The significance of the differences were computed by the Chi Square test from the frequencies in these tables.

There was hardly any difference in attitude between long-term and short-term residents in either Westgate or Westgate West. This is hardly surprising, because the statements of attitude toward the organization did frequently go beyond its utility for the respondent, "It's all right for people who want it," or, even more specific, "It's a good thing for the people who are going to stay longer."

Table 15.—Relation Between Expected Length of Stay and Attitude-Activity For Westgate West

a. ATTITUDE*

Expected Stay (months)	Favorable	Neutral, apathetic, unfavorable
0– 1	15	5
2– 5	13	2
6–13	41	12
14 plus	62	11
MEDIAN (months)	13	12

b. ACTIVITY†

	Active leader	Active follower	Inactive
0– 1	1	10	11
2– 5		7	9
6–13	10	22	20
14 plus	18	35	21
MEDIAN (months)	17	13	12

* X² not significant. Five uncategorized.
† X² (3×2 table)=11.09; $p=.05$. Two uncategorized.

The breakdown by activity tells a different story. In Westgate again little difference was found. The shortest time group—those moving out in June—could not be affected by any medium or long-range program of the Council. In spite of this, nine out of sixteen cooperated with the Council. The group expecting the longest residence—who intended to stay at least for a year and were frequently indefinite about how much longer—cooperated even a little less with the Council; only fourteen out of twenty-nine fell into these categories. The differences are not statistically significant.

In the activity ratings of the Westgate West residents, however, we find that length of expected residence made a difference. Fifty per cent of the short-term residents were actively cooperating with the Council, while 72 per cent of the long-term residents were. The median expected residence for the active leaders was seventeen months, for the inactive residents twelve months. These differences are significant at the 5 per cent level.

We thus find our derivation borne out. The data support our hypotheses concerning the difference between Westgate and Westgate West. In Westgate West, where individuals were reacting more or less independently in terms of their own needs and preferences we find a significant and appreciable degree of relationship between how much longer they expected to stay in the project and whether or not they became active in the affairs of the tenants' organization. In Westgate group influences were important. A major determinant of an individual's activity was whether or not others in his group were active. There was, consequently, no relationship at all between how long one expected to stay there, or how much benefit one would derive from the organizational activities, and whether or not one became active. We may reaffirm our hypotheses with somewhat more confidence now and look for the next testable derivation which we can make.

To be able to create and maintain group standards, a group must have power over its members. This power, the ability to induce forces on its members, stems from its cohesiveness. If the group uses this power to make the members think and act in the same way, that is, if there are group standards, the homogeneity of the attitude and activity patterns should be related to the cohesiveness of the group. Correspondingly, if no relation exists between cohesiveness and homogeneity of the pattern, the group does not use its power to induce the members to conform and we may take it as indicative of the absence of group standards.

A detailed, theoretical treatment of cohesiveness will be given later (Chapter 9), but we shall discuss the concept here in so far as it is related to the measurement employed.

The power of a group may be measured by the attractiveness of the group for the members. If a person wants to stay in a group, he will be susceptible to influences coming from the group, and he will be willing to conform to the rules which the group sets up.

The courts and buildings in Westgate and Westgate West were mainly social groups. The attractiveness of the group may, therefore, be measured by the friendships formed within the group. If residents had most of their friends within the court, the group was more attractive to them than if they had few friends within the court. The former situation will imply a more cohesive court which should be able to induce stronger forces on its members. This should result in greater homogeneity within the more cohesive court than within the less cohesive one.

The necessary measures for determining the relationship between the cohesiveness of the court and the effectiveness of the group standard are easily obtained. The sociometric data from the question regarding who the residents saw most of socially, which have already been discussed in Chapter 3, may be used here. Thus, if the members of one court give a total of 30 choices, 18 of which are given to others in their own court, the percentage of "in-court" choices is sixty. This court is then considered more cohesive than some other court which gives a total of 32 choices, only 16 of which are to others in the same court. The homogeneity of the court or how effective the group standard is may be measured simply by the percentage of members of the court who deviate from the court pattern. The more effective the group standard and the more homogeneous the court, the lower will be the percentage of members who deviate. The second and third

Table 16.—Cohesiveness of Court and Strength of Group Standard (Westgate)

Court and N of residents		% Deviates	Choices in court ——————————— Total choice	Choices in court −½ pairs ——————————— Total choice
Tolman	13	23	.62	.529
Howe	13	23	.63	.500
Rotch	8	25	.55	.523
Richards	7	29	.47	.433
Main	7	29	.67	.527
Freeman	13	38	.48	.419
Williams	13	46	.53	.447
Miller	13	46	.56	.485
Carson	13	54	.48	.403
R.O. correlation with % deviates			−.53	−.74
t^*			1.65	2.92
p			.15	.02

* Testing significance of rank order correlation as suggested by Kendall, M. G., *The Advanced Theory of Statistics*. London: Charles Griffin and Co., Limited, Vol. I, p. 401, 1943.

columns of Tables 16 and 17 show the percentage of deviates and the proportion of "in-court" choices for each court in Westgate and for each building in Westgate West.

From our hypotheses concerning the existence of group standards in the Westgate courts and the absence of group standards in the Westgate West buildings we would expect to find an appreciable negative correlation in Westgate and no correlation in Westgate West between the percentage of deviates and the proportion of "in-court" choices. In Table 16 it may be seen that the correlation is −.53 in Westgate. Here, the more cohesive the

Table 17.—Cohesiveness of Building and Strength of Group Standard (Westgate West)

Building	% Deviates	Choices in building	Choices in building—½ pairs
		Total choices	Total choices
211-20	10	.58	.50
221-30	10	.66	.59
201-10	11	.60	.54
231-40	20	.80	.64
241-50	20	.70	.61
251-60	20	.74	.63
281-90	20	.80	.68
311-20	20	.66	.53
261-70	25	.57	.46
271-80	30	.47	.38
341-50	30	.62	.50
351-60	30	.85	.76
321-30	33	.62	.52
361-70	40	.67	.56
291-300	50	.59	.50
301-10	50	.72	.64
331-40	70	.42	.35
R. O. correlation with % deviates		−.20	−.27
t		.79	1.09
p		not significant	

court (that is, the greater the proportion of "in-court" choices), the smaller the proportion of people who deviated from the court standard. As we expected, this correlation is virtually zero in Westgate West (Table 17). Here the proportion of people who deviated from the building pattern had little or nothing to do with the cohesiveness of the building group.

The measure of cohesiveness which we have used may, however, be considerably improved. The major uncertainty in the measure, as it stands, lies in our inability to distinguish between the cohesiveness of the whole group and the cohesiveness of subgroups. For example, a group of eight people all making choices within the group might or might not have high cohesiveness as a total group. As an extreme illustration, there conceivably might be two subgroups of four people each, every member within each subgroup choosing every other member but without any choices at all between the subgroups. In this case each of the subgroups may have great cohesiveness but the cohesiveness of the group as a whole would be low. Similarly, if in a group of eight or ten people there is a subgroup of three, the total group would be less cohesive than if no subgroup existed. A possible exception to this will be indicated in Chapter 7. It appears that if a strongly knit subgroup includes a large majority of the group, the cohesiveness of the whole group may still be high.

This effect of tendencies toward subgroup formation may be taken into account in our measure by correcting for the number of mutual choices which occurred. If there were no tendencies at all toward subgroup formation within a group, then the number of mutual choices which we would expect to occur would be quite low. In a group of ten people with each person giving, say, two choices within the group, we would only expect to obtain two mutual choices in the complete absence of tendencies toward subgroup or pair formation. As the tendencies toward subgroup formation increase, we will expect to find more and more mutual choices. Thus, the existence of mutual choices to some extent decreases the cohesiveness of the group as a whole. This is substantiated in a study of a Canadian veterans community,[4] where

---

[4] Infield, H. F., "A Veterans Cooperative Land Settlement and Its Sociometric Structure." *Sociometry*, Vol. 10, pp. 50-70, 1947.

it was found that stratification and class formation, a kind of subgroup development, begin to occur as soon as mutual choices develop.

It is, of course, impossible in the absence of more empirical data to decide just how much such excess mutual choices detract from the cohesiveness of the group as a whole. The proportion of mutual choices which should be subtracted from the measure of cohesiveness should, of course, be somewhere between zero and 1.00. We would not want to subtract the mutual choices completely since the fact that they are mutual certainly does not completely nullify their contribution to the cohesiveness of the group. As an approximation, we shall correct the proportion of "in-court" choices by subtracting, from the numerator of the fraction, one-half of the number of mutual choice pairs which occurred. Thus, if a court made 20 "in-court" choices 8 of which (four pairs) were mutual, we shall substract two from the twenty. If this court made a total of 36 choices, the corrected measure of cohesiveness for this court would be .50.

If the correction thus derived does actually improve the measure of cohesiveness we would expect it now to show a higher degree of relationship with the effectiveness of the group standard, that is, the percentage of deviates. The last column of Tables 16 and 17 shows these corrected measures of cohesiveness for Westgate and Westgate West respectively. It may be seen that the corrected measure does actually improve this correlation to an appreciable degree. The corrected measure of cohesiveness shows a correlation with the percentage of deviates of $-.74$. In Westgate West, of course, where we have concluded that no group standards existed, there is no reason to expect that a better measure of cohesiveness will show any more relationship to the percentage of deviates than did the first measure. In Table 17 it is clear that the change in the correlation produced by the correction is negligible. There still exists no appreciable relationship in Westgate West between cohesiveness and the number of people who deviated from the building pattern.

COHESIVENESS AND PRESTIGE

Up to this point we have been treating the courts and the buildings in the two housing projects as though each were a completely separate group. Actually, of course, in spite of the fact that the majority of friendships were formed within the court or building, there was still a fair amount of contact among courts. All courts gave some choices to other courts and received choices from other courts, and the same was true of the Westgate West buildings. In fact, there were even a very small number of choices exchanged between Westgate and Westgate West. It is possible to regard each of the courts and each of the buildings as potentially more or less cohesive subgroups which formed within the larger social structure of the housing project.

We have seen that the internal cohesiveness of these subgroups had an important bearing on the patterning of attitudes and behavior within the subgroup. It is also interesting to inquire about the way in which this cohesiveness affected the relations among the subgroups. What was the relationship, if any, between the cohesiveness of a subgroup and its "status" in the social structure? Were very cohesive subgroups more attractive to outsiders merely by virtue of the fact that they were cohesive?

One aspect of such status or prestige position is certainly the degree to which outsiders desire membership in the subgroup. Let us consider an example of a possible relationship between two subgroups. Subgroup A, on a sociometric test, may choose members of subgroup B five times while subgroup B chooses members of subgroup A fifteen times. This excess of choices which subgroup A receives from subgroup B is certainly an indication of how much more attractive subgroup A is to members of subgroup B than subgroup B is to members of subgroup A.

In other words, it may be taken as an indication of the extent to which the members of one group would like to belong to the other group. For each court in Westgate and for each building in Westgate West this measure of prestige, namely, the ratio of choices received from outsiders to choices given to outsiders, has been calculated. These scores are shown in the second column

Table 18.—*The Relation Between Cohesiveness and Prestige* (Westgate)

Court N		Outside choices received / Outside choices given	Choices in court / Total choices	Choices in court − ½ pairs / Total choices
Miller	13	.80	.56	.485
Carson	13	.81	.48	.403
Richards	7	.88	.47	.433
Freeman	13	1.06	.48	.419
Williams	13	1.06	.53	.447
Main	7	1.17	.67	.527
Howe	13	1.23	.63	.500
Rotch	8	1.30	.55	.523
Tolman	13	2.08	.62	.529
R. O. correlation with prestige measure			.53	.75
t			1.65	3.00
p			.15	.02

of Tables 18 and 19. The rank order correlations with our two measures of the cohesiveness of the court or building are shown at the bottom of the next two columns of these tables.

The correlation of the proportion of "in-court" choices with the measure of prestige of the court in Westgate is .53, which would indicate that the more cohesive courts seemed more attractive to outsiders. In Westgate West this correlation is very close to zero. The absence of any correlation in Westgate West is not surprising since we have already seen that the Westgate West buildings had really not formed into cohesive social units as yet. The possibility that the obtained correlation in Westgate was due

Table 19.—*The Relation Between Cohesiveness and Prestige* (Westgate West)

Building	Outside choices received / Outside choices given	Choices in court / Total choices	Choices in court—½ pairs / Total choices
211-220	.45	.58	.50
251-260	.50	.74	.63
281-290	.60	.80	.68
321-330	.62	.62	.52
361-370	.67	.67	.56
291-300	.75	.59	.50
271-280	.78	.47	.38
201-210	.80	.60	.54
221-230	.80	.66	.59
261-270	.90	.57	.46
341-350	.90	.62	.50
311-320	1.00	.66	.53
331-340	1.00	.42	.35
231-240	1.20	.80	.64
301-310	1.29	.72	.64
241-250	1.43	.70	.61
351-360	2.50	.85	.76
R. O. correlation with prestige measure		.24	.23
t		.96	.92
p		not significant	

to the personal attractiveness of individual members of the group rather than to the attractiveness of the group as a whole seems unlikely, since such an individual factor would be found to operate as much in Westgate West as in Westgate. It was, apparently, the attractiveness of the Westgate Court as such which bore this relation to cohesiveness.

We may check further on whether this relationship was a property of the group as a whole or not. The corrected measure of cohesiveness obtained by subtracting half of the number of mutual pairs of choices is certainly meaningful only as a measure of the group as a whole. The fact that mutual choices occurred certainly does not detract from the personal attractiveness of the individuals involved in these mutual choices. We should then expect the correlation with the measure of prestige of the sub-group to increase when the corrected measure of cohesiveness is used. This correlation in Westgate is .75, representing an appreciable increase in relationship. In Westgate West, where the buildings did not constitute really functional social units, the correlation remains unchanged—still very close to zero.

Summary

In order to conclude that observed uniformity in behavior of a number of individuals is the result of the operation of group standards or the existence of "social norms," we must be able to show the existence of psychological groups which are enforcing such standards. A collection of individuals with a relatively high number of sociometric linkages among them may constitute such a psychological group, or may merely constitute a series of friendship relationships with no real unification of the group as a whole. It is highly likely, of course, that such a series of friendship relationships among a number of people will in time make for the development of a cohesive group. In Westgate West, where there had not been time for this process really to develop, evidence indicating the absence of group standards was found.

When a cohesive group does exist, and when its realm of concern extends over the area of behavior in which we have discovered uniformity among the members of the group, then the degree of uniformity must be related to the degree of cohesiveness of the group if a group standard is operative. The more cohesive the group, the more effectively it can influence its members. Thus we have found that in the more cohesive groups in Westgate there were fewer deviates from the group pattern of behavior. The cohesiveness of the court group as a whole was the important determinant of the number of deviates. Subgroup formation within the larger group, no matter how cohesive these subgroups may have been, tended to disrupt the cohesiveness of the larger unit.

We have shown that the cohesiveness of the court is an important determinant of the social status of a court and of how effectively the court can maintain a group standard or group norm. The process by which such standards develop, however, has not been treated. In order for such standards to be developed and maintained and for them to result in uniform behavior of the group members, there must be an active process of communication concerning these matters within these groups. Some indications of the operation of this process of communication have been given in this chapter. More light will be thrown upon it during the consideration of the position of the deviate and the means by which a deviate status can be maintained in a social group.

6

The Social Status of the Deviate

WHAT are the conditions which produce deviates? When pressures and influences are being exerted on people to adopt a certain way of thinking or a certain pattern of behavior some people conform quite readily, while others are able entirely to resist these influences. The mere knowledge that these "individual differences" exist does not explain the reasons for them or the factors which are responsible for producing deviates. To learn this, we must examine the means by which group influences may be resisted.

The pressure which a group exerts on its members may be overt and sometimes even formalized. Laws, rules, mores, etiquette, and so on exemplify some of these overt pressures. The pressures which induce men to open doors for women, to dress in certain special ways on certain special occasions, or to enter their father's business are all overt and recognized. It is likely, of course, that before a group norm or standard can become thus openly formalized it must be in existence for a long time, or else must be of such a nature that deviation from the standard is harmful to the group. Such open pressures are generally also accompanied by open punishment for deviation in the form of censure, overt disapproval, or even rejection from the group.

On the other hand, the pressures which a group exerts on its members may be subtle and difficult to locate. The weight of others' opinions, the gradual change in one's ideas of what is the "normal" thing to do simply because everyone else does it, the mutual influences of people who share their ideas and their attitudes also serve effectively as pressures toward conformity with the behavior pattern of the group. Under these circumstances the consequences of nonconformity are also more subtle. These consequences may merely be a tendency to prefer those people who are not "different."

There is no indication that, in Westgate, there was any overt or formalized pressure on court members to conform to the court standard. Many of the residents realized that the people in their court were different from the people in some other court, but the influences which created and maintained these differences among courts were indirect and nonovert. Members of the courts were being influenced in their opinions and behavior merely by virtue of their association with others in their courts, without any formalized "group intent" to influence.

The strength of the influence which the group can exert in this manner depends partly upon the attractiveness of the group for the member and partly on the degree to which the member is in communication with others in the group. No matter how attractive the group is to a particular person it will be impossible for the group to exert any influence on him if he is never in communication with the group. We may now examine some of the conditions under which individuals will be able to resist these influences.

1. The group may not be sufficiently attractive to the member. Under these circumstances the relatively weak influence which the group exerts cannot overcome personal considerations which may happen to be contrary to the group standard. Some examples will illustrate this phenomenon:

(*Mr. and Mrs. C. in Williams Court*)   We don't have any opinion at all about the organization. We're bad ones for you to interview; we have no need for an organization because we're pretty happy at home. We're socially self-sufficient. Others in the court felt it was wonderful and they discovered many that felt that way. We have friends in this and other courts but our main interests are in the home.

(*Mr. and Mrs. K. in Tolman Court*) We think the organization is sort of silly. It isn't necessary for a group like this. We've gone to meetings because our court likes it and is very active. Our friends now are spread all over pretty much. We used to have a nice group here but several moved away. We see a lot of the people in our court now but we aren't too friendly except with one or two.

2. There may not be sufficient communication between the member and others in the group. Under these conditions the pressures from the group are simply not brought to bear on the member although, if they had been exerted, they might have been very effective. In such instances the deviate may not even be aware of the fact that he is different from most of the others in his group. Examples of this type of deviate are:

(*Mr. and Mrs. S. in Freeman Court*) The organization is a good idea but the trouble with people like us is that we don't have time. That's why we haven't had anything to do with it. I think it's the consensus of opinion that people here don't have the time. [Actually the majority of the people in the court were active.] There are wonderful people living here but it seems peculiar to Westgate that people are hard to get to know. A lot of people come here expecting to make friends without any trouble and then find it isn't so easy. It would be a good thing if the organization helped people to get acquainted.

(*Mr. and Mrs. Z. in Miller Court*) We don't have much time for things like the tenants' organization and haven't had anything to do with it. Some are active and others aren't. There aren't any particular people we are particularly friendly with. Everyone is in the same boat though and people are generally friendly. It's been very nice living here and the people are nice too. We live on the corner though, and seem to get left out of a lot of things because of that.

3. The influence of some other group to which the people belong may be stronger than the influence which the court group

is able to exert on them. Under these conditions the person who appears as a deviate is a deviate only because we have chosen, somewhat arbitrarily, to call him a member of the court group. He does deviate from his own court, but he conforms to some other group to which he actually feels he belongs. Such a group may of course, be outside of Westgate all together. There are instances, however, of people belonging to groups other than their own court but still within the limits of Westgate:

(*Mr. and Mrs. M. in Carson Court*) We think the organization is fine and Mrs. M. is the chairman of the social committee which is holding its first big event tomorrow night. I don't see much of the others in this court. My real friends are in the next court over there, in Tolman Court. There are only two people living in this court that do anything for the organization, myself and one other person. It's generally understood that the others have different interests. The people in Tolman Court are more active. Carson Court people aren't as sociable as people in Tolman Court.

(*Mr. and Mrs. N. in Howe Court*) We think the organization is a really splendid idea but to be truthful we haven't been active in it. The others in this court don't think much of it and I don't think our court even has a representative. Our friends aren't confined to this court at all. They are scattered all over Westgate. Actually, only a very small proportion of our friends live in this court. Our friends are mainly people with the same interests and backgrounds that we have.

The Deviate in Westgate

These three types of conditions do, then, appear to produce deviates; at least we were able to locate deviates who seemed to exhibit such patterns of relationship between themselves and the group. If these are the major factors which make for nonconformity we should also be able to demonstrate their relevance for all of the deviates rather than for a few selected examples. The two variables, attractiveness of the group for the member and amount of communication between the member and the group, should be reflected in the sociometric choices which people gave and received. We should expect that deviates would give fewer choices to others in their court and would receive fewer choices from them. Whether this happened because they were not in full communication with the group or because the group was not attractive to them, the result in the sociometric choices should be essentially the same—the deviates should be sociometric isolates in their court.

Table 20 shows the average number of "in-court" choices given

Table 20.—*Average Number of "In-Court" Choice of Deviates and Conformers in Westgate*

	N	Choices given	Choices received
Deviates	36	1.25	1.11
Conformers	64	1.53	1.61

and received by the 36 deviates and the 64 conformers in Westgate. It is readily apparent that the deviates were more isolated, sociometrically, than were the conformers. They both gave and received fewer choices than did the conformers.[1] Moreover, the conformers tended to receive more choices than they gave, while the deviates tended to receive fewer choices than they gave. Deviates tended to choose conformers more than conformers chose deviates. This might be called relative rejection by the conformers.

Deviate status, then, was accompanied by a smaller degree of association with others in the court. It is still possible, however,

---

[1] The significance of the differences in this and the following tables was computed by taking the means for each court and comparing the distributions of these means. This was done because the effects of group standards made the group, not the individual, the unit of sampling. This difference is significant at the 7 per cent level of confidence for choices given. Significance is at the 17 per cent level of confidence for choices received.

that these deviates were not true isolates, but merely members of groups other than the court group. In our case studies we saw two examples of this sort. An examination of all sociometric choices exchanged with people outside the court, however, reveals that this was not true of the deviates as a whole. Table 21

Table 21.—*Average Number of "Out-Court" Choices of Deviates and Conformers in Westgate*

	N	Choices given	Choices received
Deviates	36	1.14	.89
Conformers	64	1.16	1.55

shows the average number of "out-court" choices given and received by the deviates and conformers. It is clear that the deviates, in the main, were not members of groups other than those of their own court. They gave only as many choices to people outside their own court as did the conformers, but received considerably fewer choices from outside than the conformers.[2] We must conclude that these deviates, who had fewer associations within their own court, also had fewer associations with others in Westgate—at least in so far as this is reflected by the number of choices they received.

Choices given by deviates to people outside their own court tended to be given to the conformers in other courts. These conformers tended not to reciprocate the choices. The deviate, who was perceived as being different from the others in his court, was not as often chosen by outsiders. This is consistent with our knowledge that the court is perceived as the basis for social grouping in Westgate. People who were on the fringes of their own group were also on the fringe of social life between courts.

[2] Significant at the 2 per cent level of confidence.

While conformers in Westgate received an average of 3.16 choices from others, the deviates received an average of only 2.00 such choices. The deviates were relative isolates. It is clear that this isolation was not wholly voluntary on the part of the deviates since they gave only slightly fewer choices than the conformers.

It is possible to examine more closely the situation of the deviate if we restrict ourselves to the six full-size courts in Westgate. It will be recalled that ten of the houses in these six courts faced onto the street rather than into the courtyard area, so that

Table 22.—Average Number of "In-Court" Choices of Deviates and Conformers for the Six Large Courts in Westgate

	N	Choices given	Choices received
Deviates in Corner house	7	.57	.43
Deviates in Inner houses	23	1.52	1.39
Conformers	48	1.52	1.60

the people living in these houses had fewer contacts with others in the court. Of the other 68 people living in these courts only 34 per cent were deviates, while seven of the 10 corner-house residents were deviates. It appears, then, that the isolated geographical position in which these 10 found themselves, and the resultant lack of contact between them and the rest of the court, made it difficult for the court to exert influence on them. The lack of contact suggests that mainly chance factors would determine whether they would show the pattern of attitude and behavior that had become the standard in the court.

Table 22 shows the "in-court" choices for these six full-size courts with the corner-house deviates separated from the others. The lack of contact between the court and the deviates in these cornerhouses is readily apparent. They both gave and received only about one-third as many choices as did the others in the court.[3] It is not surprising that they had remained uninfluenced by the group standard in their particular court.

The other deviates in the court did not suffer from such lack of contact. They gave as many choices to the others in the court as did the conformers. As was true for all the deviates in Westgate, however, they tended to receive fewer than they gave, while the conformers tended to receive more choices then they gave.[4]

Table 23.—*Average Number of "Out-Court" Choices of Deviates and Conformers for the Six Large Westgate Courts*

	N	Choices given	Choices received
Deviates in Corner house	7	1.29	1.14
Deviates in Inner houses	23	1.13	.87
Conformers	48	1.17	1.58

Table 23 again shows that these inner-house deviates were not members of groups other than the court group. They gave only as many choices to people outside their own court as did the conformers and, again, received many fewer.

The deviates stood out as relative isolates, not only within their own court, but in Westgate as a whole. The corner-house deviates received, from all sources, an average of only 1.57 choices, the other deviates received an average of 2.26 choices, while the conformers received an average of 3.18 choices. The conformers were more closely involved with the social life in

[3] For all comparisons this is significant at at least the 3 per cent level of confidence.
[4] Not statistically significant.

Westgate than were the deviates. Whether relative isolation brings about deviate status (as seems to be the case for those living in corner houses) or whether deviate status tends to bring about isolation through "rejection by others" (as might be the case with the deviates living in inner houses) the two things seem to go hand in hand.

THE DEVIATE IN WESTGATE WEST

We concluded in the previous chapter that there was no relation in Westgate West between the uniformity of behavior within a building and the cohesiveness of the building, that group standards were not operating in Westgate West. The opinions of the people about the tenants' organization and their degree of activity in it would, consequently, not be determined by pressures or influences from the group. The behavior of the individual would be more a matter of individual reaction and influence from other individuals than of group pressures.

We may well examine the sociometric status of those people who were different from the majority in their building, although we should not expect the isolation which we found among the deviates in Westgate. These people were deviates only in the sense that they reacted differently from most of the residents and not in the sense of having successfully resisted group pressures to conform.

Few people in Westgate West expressed unfavorable attitudes toward the organization. Consequently, few people differed from the pattern of their building on the attitude dimension. The great majority of the deviates differed only on the activity dimension from the others in their building. Thirteen of the seventeen buildings had "favorable-active" patterns, and most of the deviates were people who felt favorably inclined but had merely not attended the meetings of their building. It is plausible to expect, then, that we would find these deviates not to be isolates in the community despite their absence from building meetings. The data presented in Table 24 corroborates these expectations. The data treat only those residents who did not live in apartment positions 2 and 4 in the Westgate West buildings. The reason for omitting the people in these two apartment positions will be discussed shortly.

Table 24.—Average Number of Choices of Deviates and Conformers Living in Apartments Other Than Numbers 2 and 4 in Westgate West

| | N | "In-building" | | "Out-building" | |
		Choices given	Choices received	Choices given	Choices received
Deviates	33	1.42	1.48	1.09	1.06
Conformers	99	1.74	1.93	.79	.75

While none of the differences between conformers and deviates in Westgate West are statistically significant, it is interesting to note the tendencies. We find, on examining this table, that the deviates gave and received fewer choices in their own building than did the conformers. Consequently, they had less connection with others in their building. Thus, it is plausible that these deviates would have been less likely to attend a building meeting. It is important to note that, since there were no pressures from the group as such, and hence no true deviation in the sense of resisting group pressures, there was no hint of "rejection" by the conformers. The deviates received fully as many choices as they gave in their own building.

While the deviates had less connection with others in their own building, they had more connection with others outside of their building. The deviates both gave and received more choices outside of their building than the conformers. This again corroborates the supposition that there was simply less motivation on the part of the deviates to attend building meetings, since their social life was centered outside of their own buildings to a larger extent. Altogether, deviates and conformers both gave an average of about two and a half choices and both received an average of about two and a half choices. We may thus conclude that, in the absence of strong group formation and in the absence of group standards, being different from the people in the group did not result in isolation.

The residents of apartment positions 2 and 4 in Westgate West are considered separately from the others because they were relatively isolated by virtue of the geographical position in which

Table 25.—*Average Number of Choices of Deviates and Conformers Living in Apartment Numbers 2 and 4 in Westgate West*

	N	"In-building"		"Out-building"	
		Choices given	Choices received	Choices given	Choices received
Deviates	15	1.53	1.07	.93	.47
Conformers	19	1.89	1.16	1.05	.84

they lived. Chapter 3 showed that the number of contacts which the residents of apartments 2 and 4 had with other residents of the building were somewhat limited. The residents of apartment number 3 had the advantage of central location and the residents of apartment numbers 1 and 5 had the advantage of contacts with upstairs people, but the residents of apartments 2 and 4 received fewer choices both on their floor and from the other floor than did the residents of any other apartment positions. The people living in apartments 2 and 4 were consequently analagous to the residents of the corner houses in Westgate, although their physical isolation was not as extreme as that of the corner-house residents. Table 25 gives the data for these people.

Examination of Table 25 shows that when physical location in the building is the cause of relative isolation, there are only slight differences between deviates and conformers. Although the deviates tended to give and receive fewer choices both inside and outside their building than did the conformers, the differences were uniformly slight. Both deviates and conformers in these two apartments were similar in receiving consistently fewer choices than they gave and, in this respect, both differed from the people who did not live in these positions.

There is also a tendency for the isolation which results from the physical position to increase the number of deviates. Forty-four per cent of the residents of apartment positions 2 and 4 were deviates while only 25 per cent of the other residents deviated from the pattern of their building. Probably, as groups form in Westgate West, and as group standards will develop there, the sociometric status of the deviates will become more and more like what was found in Westgate.

The Relation of the Deviate to the Larger Community

Up to this point we have considered the social status of the deviate only within the housing project community. We have found that in Westgate, where group standards existed, the deviate was sociometrically isolated. We suggested earlier, however, that the social life of the deviates may have centered outside of Westgate. Whether such greater emphasis on social life outside of Westgate was a cause or a result of their isolated position in Westgate cannot be determined.

Data which determine whether a relationship exists were gathered in an interview with 40 of the Westgate residents (Chapter 2). There are data concerning both outside friendships and deviate status on only the 34 of these 40 people who still lived in Westgate at the time when the latter data were gathered. Twelve of these 34 people were deviates from their courts. From this material it was possible to determine whether the social life of these people centered mainly in Westgate or mainly outside of Westgate. Table 26 shows that a relationship did exist between the locus of their social life and their deviate status. Of the 18 people whose social life was judged to center mainly in Westgate, only three proved to be deviates. Of the sixteen people whose social life tended to center outside of Westgate, nine were deviates. It is reasonable to suppose that for those people whose

Table 26.—The Locus of the Social Life of Deviates and Conformers in Westgate*

	Conformers	Deviates
Social life centered in Westgate	15	3
Social life not centered in Westgate	7	9

* Chi Square significant at 2 per cent level of confidence. Data from the interview of July, 1946.

social life centered outside of Westgate, the court was less important and less attractive. They would, then, be more able to resist influences which this group exerted on them.

Although, on the basis of the data available to us, we have not been able clearly to separate the different means by which people can resist group influences and thus become deviates, there is abundant evidence that the attractiveness of the group and the amount of communication between the member and the group are major determinants. It also would seem likely that these two factors would generally not occur separately but would operate together in most situations. The sociometric status of the deviate is clearly different from that of the conformer—isolation seems to be both a cause and an effect of being a deviate.

7

The Process of Communication

DETAILED knowledge concerning the process of communication among people, and the factors affecting various aspects of this communication, is essential for a thorough consideration of group functioning and of the relations between individuals and social groups. Such communication, verbal or otherwise, is, after all, the means by which one individual influences another, the means by which groups function effectively together, and the means by which the general process of social existence is made possible. In the preceding two chapters, for example, we have stressed how the process of communication among people determines the growth of group standards concerning the attitudes and behavior of these people on matters relevant to the functioning of the social group to which they belong.

Much of the discussion concerning the importance of communication in the functioning of groups has been on a theoretical level. Thus the hypothesis has been advanced that a friendship between two people implies the existence of an active channel of communication between them; that is, information and opinions relevant to immediate social behavior of the people will flow from one to the other. In line with this hypothesis, we used data obtained by means of a sociometric question in an interview to reveal such channels of communication in a social group. We also hypothesized that the process of communication, and its effects in making people think and act similarly, were responsible for the observed group standards about the Westgate tenants' organization.

By directly studying the process of communication much can be learned about the exact way in which this process functions in affecting group life. There are at least three problems concerning the process of communication which are important in explaining the results of group standards in Westgate. These three problems are:

1. What content will and what will not be communicated in a social group? If the process of communication is responsible for the formation of similar attitudes and similar behavior among people in a social group, then the factors which determine what content will or will not be communicated are the same factors which will determine the aspects of behavior about which the group does or does not develop standards. If there is very little communication about political questions, for example, it is quite unlikely, according to our theory, that the group will develop group standards on such issues. If there is a great deal of communication concerning new styles in women's clothes it is extremely likely that a group standard will arise on this matter.

2. To whom will things be communicated? Some of the data presented in previous chapters tend to show that people will be affected by group standards to the extent that these people are part of the communication process. The specific factors which make for one person's hearing about something while another does not hear about it are consequently important in determining degrees of group membership and the extent of influence by group standards.

3. What affects the acceptance of a communication? A given item, when communicated to another person, may or may not be accepted by that person; hence it may or may not change his opinions or his way of looking at things. To the extent that communications are accepted, these communications are effective in

furthering the development of group cohesion and group stand-ards. Although little work has been done on these problems, there is evidence to give us better understanding of this process. The problem of communication is of such vital importance for under-standing group functioning that the suggestive data which are available are worthy of consideration.

THE METHODOLOGY OF STUDYING SPREAD OF INFORMATION

In Westgate information was planted deliberately in order to study, in a relatively controlled way, the determinants of com-munication. The experiment was set up so that one could spe-cifically observe the effect of certain factors which were felt to be important. The general plan of the study was to plant dis-tinguishable, yet comparable, items of information which were favorable to the tenants' organization—one in a court which had a favorable group standard, and the other in a court which had an unfavorable group standard. A subsequent thorough study of how each of these items of information spread and to whom they spread, would shed light on some of the determinants of such communication. We would be able to observe the effect of attitude toward the organization on the extent of spread of such favorable information. The selection of the material to be planted was guided by several considerations:

1. The information had to be new and such that it could not come from other sources; otherwise the tracing of spread might be difficult.

2. The material had to be such that it would not disrupt in any way the activities going on in the housing project. This type of consideration is vital in any experiments on natural groups.

3. It had to be plausible material which could be accepted by the residents as true. If it were not believed, it would probably not spread and the study would be worthless.

4. The material had to be of enough interest so that it would

spread sufficiently. Unfortunately, in setting up such experiments it is necessary to know in advance the probable answers to the questions one is asking in order for the experiment to be successful. Thus, one of the objectives of the study was to find out if favorable information would or would not spread more from the favorable than from the unfavorable court. To make certain that some spread would occur, however, part of the answer to this question had to be known. In laboratory experiments the usual course of procedure is to conduct some tentative or preliminary studies before the final experiment is standardized. In field experiments this is almost impossible. One must rely on such intimate knowledge of the community as can be gained from intensive formal and informal observation, and one must depend on a guiding theory.

5. It was also necessary to have material of such a nature that two equivalent versions, which were nevertheless distinct enough to be separated when tracing the spread, could be planted in separate courts.

The information finally selected seemed to satisfy these various conditions. In the favorable-active court, Tolman, the story was planted that a popular magazine, with national distribution, was going to run a feature article about the Westgate Council as a good example of such activities in veterans' housing projects. In the unfavorable-inactive court, Howe, the story was planted that a program with the same content would be broadcast on a national radio network.

The two courts selected for planting the story were as different as possible in terms of attitude towards the organization and participation in it, but were similar with respect to other factors. Tolman Court, where the magazine story was planted, had a favorable-active group standard from which only three of the thirteen residents deviated. Howe Court, where the radio story was planted, had an unfavorable-inactive group standard from which, also, three of the thirteen residents deviated. The co-hesiveness of the two courts as measured by the percentage of their sociometric choices given inside their own court were quite similar. The residents of Tolman Court gave 21 sociometric choices inside their court and 13 outside. The residents of Howe Court gave 22 choices inside and 13 outside their own court. There is a difference between them, however, in the number of times residents were chosen from the outside. Tolman Court residents received 27 choices from outside while Howe Court residents received only 16 choices. There is thus some indication that Tolman Court had more contact with other courts than did Howe Court.

The stories were planted in the two courts at the same time, and the method of planting the story was chosen so as to give the greatest chance of having the material accepted as true by the residents of the project. A woman, posing as a reporter for a well-known magazine, went to the favorable-active court, Tolman, and interviewed two women in their homes. A man posing as a reporter for a broadcasting company, went to the unfavorable-inactive court, Howe, and interviewed two women in their homes. In both courts each interview lasted about twenty minutes. Because of the necessity for simultaneity in planting the information in the two courts, and because of the difficulty of finding people at home, the persons with whom the information was to be planted were selected as follows: Two people in each court were chosen at random and for each of them several alternates were also chosen. These selections were given to the "reporters," who were not familiar with the project or its residents. The following excerpts from the reports of these two people give a picture of how the stories were planted and how they were received by the residents.

I stopped first at number ten. Someone was there and I said that I was from ——— magazine and that we were having a series of articles about veterans and their living conditions, and that we wanted to do a picture story on this particular housing project and its activities in a community-wide sense. I asked her to tell me something about the kinds of function that have been sponsored by the tenants' organization. She told me about the Easter egg hunt, the splash party, the picnics that were planned for the summer. She also said her husband was chairman of the economics committee that went around asking cleaners for their rates. She was extremely nice and cordial, and went on in great detail about the things the organization had done, the kinds of people living in the project, ideas that would make for good pictures, and the general setup of the project.

The next woman that I found at home was at number eighteen. I told her essentially the same thing about the purpose of the interview and told her about some of the information which the first person had given. She reiterated many of the same things. Again the woman was cordial and cooperative, and we spent about twenty minutes discussing the various aspects of the activities of the tenants' organization which might make a good story.

The man supposedly from the broadcasting company describes his two interviews as follows:

I went first to number fifty-six and knocked at the door. The woman in number fifty-seven told me that she didn't think I would find anyone home there. I told her that I was just trying to interview some people in the community and wondered if I could talk to her for a few minutes. [Number 57 was listed as an alternate for number 56.] She very kindly invited me in and we sat and talked for about twenty minutes. I told her that we were planning to work up a program to be presented over the ———— radio network about the Westgate community and particularly about the tenants' organization which I understood was called Westgate Council. She was very pleasant and very willing to tell me anything she could about the community and about her life there, but she said that she didn't know very much about the Council and displayed some embarrassment because of this. She talked in great detail about the people in Westgate and life in Westgate, but knew little and expressed very little interest in the organization and its activities.

I then went to number fifty-three. When I told the woman who answered what I wanted, she very pleasantly asked me in. We sat down and talked for about twenty minutes. I explained about the radio program for which I was gathering information and asked her about the community organization and what it had been doing. She explained that their court was quite indifferent to the organization. She indicated that when the organization was formed they had answered a questionnaire and had by no means opposed it. They had, however, not been interested in participating in its activities.

The evening of the day following the planting of this information, interviewing was started to ascertain the extent and direction of spread. The interviewing was done in the evening, since that seemed to be the best time to find the tenants at home. It was concluded in two evenings and ninety of the hundred families were reached. The interview included questions designed to ascertain whether or not the people had heard the information, from whom they had heard it, whether they had told it to anyone else and, if so, to whom. The question used to determine whether or not they had heard either of the items of information was, "Have you heard of any publicity that the tenants' organization is getting?"

The most serious drawback in the data collected about the communication of these two items of information was the unexpected inadequacy of this question for determining whether or not the information had been heard. The results obtained undoubtedly underestimate the extent of the spread of the information. There are two clear-cut bases for this assertion of the inadequacy of the question. One of the four people with whom the information was planted, number 18 Tolman Court, gave no indication, when interviewed later, of having heard anything about it. The response to the question was "no," and non-directive probing failed to elicit any further information. On the last evening of interviewing, when there was no longer the possibility of the interviewing itself causing spread which would affect our results, the interviewer probed additionally by saying, "We have heard there has been talk about a story in some magazine or on the radio. Did you hear anything about that?" Two persons, after having answered "no" to the original question, gave clear evidence of having heard one of the items of information when the direct question was asked. In spite of this inadequacy it was possible, on the basis of the responses to the various questions, to reconstruct the spread of the information. It must be kept in mind, however, that there may have been others who heard the information but are not included in our reconstruction.

It is interesting to note the way in which the execution of this experimental study depended upon the information gathered by means of observation and interviewing. The data collected in the Westgate housing project had indicated the existence of fairly strong group standards in each court relevant to the tenants' organization and rather marked differences in the standards between one court and another. The theoretical explanation of this state of affairs rested on the hypothesis that such group standards were developed through communication among the members of a group on relevant matters. This theoretical explanation implies that there would be little or no communication on matters relevant to the tenants' organization between members of courts which had widely different group standards. It was consequently indicated that an experimental study of communication would be fruitful in checking this hypothesis and in studying more intimately the process involved.

Detailed knowledge of the state of affairs in the Westgate community was necessary in order to set up the experiment. It was necessary to know what the group standards in the various courts were so that two widely different ones could be chosen for the planting of the information. It was also necessary to know a good deal about the composition of the courts so that the two which were chosen would be equated in other respects, thus leaving our experimental variable relatively uncomplicated. It was further necessary to know fairly intimately what the organization was about and the state of its development so that a proper selection of information to be planted could be made and a reasonable way of planting this information devised.

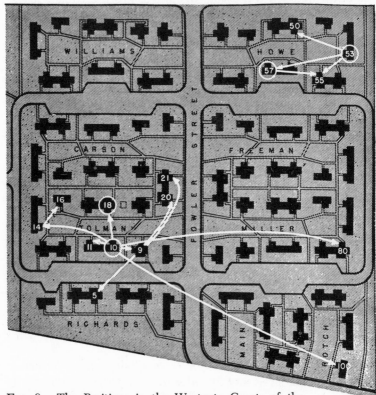

FIG. 8. The Positions in the Westgate Courts of the People Who Heard and Told Either of the Two Items of Information

THE SPREAD OF INFORMATION IN WESTGATE

The details of the spread of the two planted items of information in the Westgate housing project are shown in Figure 8. This figure shows the nine Westgate courts in their approximate geographical positions, and the positions in the courts of the people who heard or told either of the two items of information. The positions of the people with whom the information was planted are encircled. The directions of the arrows indicate the direction of the communication. Thus, for example, in the unfavorable-inactive court, Howe, where the radio story was planted, number 53, one of those with whom it was planted, told three people about it, one of whom was number 57, the other person with whom the information was planted. In the favorable-active court, Tolman, where the magazine story was used, number 10, with whom the story was planted, communicated the story to number 9, who in turn repeated it to three other people.

There are a number of facts which are immediately apparent upon examining Figure 8. The patterns of spread of the two stories are different. The story planted in the unfavorable-inactive court spread to very few people while the story planted in the favorable-active court spread to a considerable number. This greater spread of the story in the favorable court exists in spite of the fact that one of the people with whom this story was planted did not communicate it to anyone. The greater spread is, in effect, the direct and indirect result of the communication of only one person. Another indication of the more active communication of the story in the favorable-active court is the fact that there were two cases in this court of relaying of information. That is, number 9 and number 14 forwarded the information to others after they heard it from number 10. In the unfavorable-inactive court there were no such occurrences. All four acts of communication were performed by the people with whom the story was originally planted. We may conclude that a much more active process of communication existed about content favorable to the tenants' organization in the favorable court than existed in the unfavorable court.

It is also interesting to note the relationship between the spread of the two items of information and the geography of Westgate.

Both stories stayed fairly close to the courts in which they were planted. In the unfavorable court the radio story stayed entirely within the court. In the favorable court, while the bulk of the communications were also within the court, there was an appreciable degree of "overflow." Two of the people to whom the communication "overflowed," numbers 5 and 21, were still geographically close to the source of the information. The other two people outside of the court to whom the information was communicated, numbers 80 and 100, were really special cases. They were, respectively, one of the founders of the tenants' organization and the current chairman of it. There was no geographical overlapping at all between the patterns of spread of the two stories. In fact, there seems to be a zone between the two courts which was completely untouched by any communications on the matter. It is, of course, quite likely that content which would provoke more communication than did these stories would have spread to this untouched zone and might even have produced some geographical overlap. It is fairly clear, though, that the amount of communication on content such as these stories decreases as the distance between people becomes greater.

THE RUMOR AT REGENT HILL

More light is thrown on the determinants of the spread of information by data obtained from a study of the spread of a rumor which arose spontaneously[1] in another community which we shall call Regent Hill.

Regent Hill was built as a low-rent housing project for the accommodation of shipyard workers during the war. It consisted of one hundred single or semi-attached houses occupying an area of about four blocks. The study was done in connection with a larger research program which involved measuring the

[1] Festinger, L., et al., "The Study of a Rumor: Its Origin and Spread," *Human Relations.* Vol. 1, pp. 464-486, 1948.

effects on the social life in a housing project of stimulating the organization of community activities. A community organizer worked with the residents of Regent Hill toward these ends. The major efforts on the part of tenants, stimulated and pushed by the community organizer, were directed towards the establishment of a cooperative nursery school in the project. While interest and involvement in the cooperative nursery school was growing, considerable resistance was also developing on the part of many residents. This resistance culminated in the appearance of a rumor, the content of which was hostile to the continued development of community activities and to the people who were stimulating them. Acceptance of the rumor would have meant the complete cessation of the activities.

It was possible to study the conditions leading to the beginning of this rumor and some of the factors which were related to its spread through the housing project. The major source of data was an intensive open-ended interview with a sample of the residents of the project some time after the rumor had died down. Questions specifically relating to the spread of this rumor were inserted in a longer interview schedule. Data were thus obtained on the factors determining the extent and direction of the spread of the rumor. The results from this study are presented below, together with comparable analyses from the Westgate experiment.

DO FRIENDSHIPS IMPLY ACTIVE CHANNELS OF COMMUNICATION?

The data from both studies tend to support the hypothesis that the existence of a friendship between two people also implies the existence of an active channel of communication. In other words, other things being equal, information is more likely to be communicated to friends than to others. Probably the existence of a friendship relationship makes it easier to communicate on a wide variety of matters.

In the study of the hostile rumor in Regent Hill, it was possible to divide the sample of people interviewed into three groups: (1) those who indicated that they had close friends living in the housing project, (2) those having many acquaintances but not very close friends, and (3) those who reported they had no friends in the project. The percentages of people in these three groups who heard the rumor were 62, 42, and 33 respectively. It appears, then, that people with close friends in the project were much more likely to have heard the rumor than those with no friends. Although the relationship obtained here is far from perfect, the data certainly tend to support the conclusion that friendships indicate active channels of communication. The information did apparently tend to flow along friendship lines.

In the Westgate study, it was possible to make a more detailed examination of the relationship between communication of the planted items of information and the friendship patterns which we knew to exist. Altogether, fourteen acts of communication of the planted information were identified in the interviewing. These acts of communication were compared with the people's sociometric choices given in response to the question, "what people in the project do you see most of socially." Six of the fourteen acts of communication corresponded exactly to these sociometric choices.

The relationship between acts of communication and friendships is shown even more clearly if we examine the matter in more detail. In the unfavorable-inactive court, Howe, three of the four acts of communication corresponded to sociometric choices. The only one which did not correspond was the communication from number 53 to number 57. It will be seen in Chapter 8 that numbers 50, 55, and 57 formed a clique in which all mutually chose each other on the sociometric question. Number 53 chose two of the people in this clique but was not chosen by any of them. With this in mind, the pattern of communication which occurred in this court becomes quite clear. Number 53 communicated to each of the people in the clique and number 57 communicated to one of the persons in the clique. The information was thus completely circulated within this small friendship grouping but did not spread to anyone else.

Of the ten acts of communication that were identified from the favorable-active court, Tolman, three corresponded with sociometric choices. Here, where there were stronger forces toward communication, the relationship with the friendship choices was far from perfect, although it again indicates that friendships provide one channel of communication for such information. Other factors come into play in determining to whom a communication is made when the force to communicate is strong enough. This will be developed in somewhat greater detail shortly, but it is worthwhile to point out here that five of the seven acts of communication that did not correspond to sociometric choices were made to people who were particularly prominent in founding or running the Westgate tenants organization.

The existence of a friendship indicates the existence of a channel for the communication of information, but other factors will undoubtedly determine whether or not that or any particular channel will be used for communication. Probably the degree to which the friendship channels of communication will be used will depend upon the relevance of a specific item of information to the functioning of the friendship group involved.

WHAT WILL AND WILL NOT BE COMMUNICATED

Although the data which we are considering present only interesting suggestions concerning this question, one general factor seems to emerge. Interest and involvement in matters relevant to the content of an item of information will be a determinant of the strength of the impulse to communicate it to others. On the basis of the data which we will present below, one can advance the more specific hypothesis that the greater the implication of a specific item of information for change in the immediate social behavior of a person, the greater will be the impulse to tell others about it.

In the study of the spread of the hostile rumor in the Regent Hill project the sample interviewed was divided into three groups on the basis of the extent of participation in the community activities with which the hostile rumor was concerned. The first group was made up of respondents who had themselves participated in these community activities. The second group was made up of respondents who had not participated themselves while others in their families had. The last group was made up of respondents who had not themselves participated, nor had anyone else in their family. The percentages of people in these three groups who, knowing about the rumor, had told it to others were 67, 54, and 0 respectively. Thus, two thirds of those who had participated in community activities were sufficiently affected by the rumor to repeat it to others; not one of those who had no connection at all with the community activities felt inclined to talk about it. It is clear that a rumor hostile to the activities affected the social behavior of those who had participated themselves and those whose families had participated in these activities. It did not at all affect the social behavior of those who had had no connection with the activities, and consequently these latter people did not transmit the rumor.

In line with this hypothesis, it might be expected that in the Westgate study the behavior of people in the favorable-active court would be affected by this information, which added to the prestige of the tenants' organization, but that it would be largely irrelevant to the behavior of the people in the unfavorable-inactive court who had little connection with the activities of the organization. We would thus expect much stronger impulses to talk about it in the favorable-active court. The data, indeed, serve to corroborate this hypothesis. The magazine publicity story planted in the favorable-active court, Tolman, was heard by nine other people in four different courts. The radio publicity story planted in the unfavorable-inactive court, Howe, was only heard by two other people, both in the same court in which the story was planted.

TO WHOM WILL A GIVEN ITEM OF INFORMATION BE COMMUNICATED?

The data from the two studies under discussion suggest that a factor similar to the one which determines whether or not there will be an impulse to spread the information also operates to determine the direction of this spread. We have seen that if an item of information affects the social behavior of the person, this person will feel impelled to talk about it and communicate this information to others. We now advance the hypothesis that the direction of spread, that is, the people to whom the information will be communicated, will be determined by the perceived relevance of this information to other people. The information is most likely to be communicated to those who are thought to be most affected by it.

In the Regent Hill study the content of the rumor was mainly concerned with the organization of a cooperative nursery school. It is plausible to suppose that the rumor would be seen as relevant to those people who had children of nursery school age. When the sample of people who were interviewed was divided into those who had children of nursery school age and those who did not have any such children, it was found that 62 per cent of the former group had heard the rumor, while only 28 per cent of the latter group had heard it. It is clear, then, that appearing likely to be affected by the content of the information was a determinant of whether or not one heard it.

Similarly, in Westgate it may plausibly be reasoned that an

item of information such as the one planted in the favorable-
active court, namely, that a nationally known magazine was
going to feature a story of the Westgate organization, would be
of most relevance for those who were most instrumental in starting the organization and those who were most active in it. The
item of information did actually spread to these key people. Of the
three people who were the original founders of the organization,
one was no longer living in Westgate, the other two were among
the nine people to whom the information was communicated.
Another two of the nine to whom the information was communicated were the chairman and the clerk of the Westgate Council.
A fifth person was the chairman of the social committee of the
Council, the most active committee at that time. Thus all of
the people who were in key positions either in the founding or the
running of the Westgate organization were recipients of this
communication. It will be recalled that the other communications were mainly determined by the existence of friendship connections. It thus becomes clear that the communication of such
information is not an amorphous affair, but is highly selective.
Communication occurs toward those who are seen as being most
affected by the information or towards those with whom communication is easiest, namely, friends.

We have seen that once a social group is formed the connections
within it also function as channels of communication along which
information and opinions flow. This process will tend to make the
social grouping more and more cohesive. There are indications
that information relevant to the immediate functioning of the
social group will be communicated more frequently than information of less relevance. The variety of things which are relevant
to the functioning of the group will thus have an important
effect on the number of different things about which the group

develops standards and about which the group exerts pressures toward conformity.

Much more must be learned about this process of communication before a coherent theory of its functioning can be developed. Studies of the acceptance of communication of opinions and of the effects of nonverbal communication are urgently needed before a comprehensive picture of this aspect of group life can be formed.

8

Patterns of Group Structure

In the study of groups by means of sociometric data much attention has been given to the exact pattern of connections among individuals. The need to describe and analyze the patterning of these connections has been apparent. It is not only important to know how many friendships exist in a group and what proportion of them are mutual friendships, but it is also important to know who a particular person's friends are, what his relations are with the friends of his friends, and what tendencies to subgroup or clique formation exist. We need to know how many paths of influence exist among members of a group, who can influence whom, over how much of a group a person's influence extends, and what is the nature of the indirect influence chains that may exist. If an item of information enters a group it is not only important to know how many people will eventually hear about it but also to know exactly who will hear it and from whom and how far removed from the original source it will be by the time a specific person hears about it.

Without an adequate representational technique of handling such data the analysis of the exact patterns of interconnections among members of a group is virtually impossible unless the group is very small. As the size of the group increases, the complexity of the pattern generally makes it difficult to comprehend by mere inspection. The result has been the relative neglect of this kind of analysis. Investigators have, by and large, contented themselves with analyzing sociometric patterns in such terms as the number of choices people receive, the kind of people who get most choices, the proportion of the choices inside the group, and other such summary measures which serve to relate the sociometric choices to other variables.

The major portion of this chapter will be devoted to the development of a method of treating sociometric choices which makes it possible to analyze more complex interrelationships. By the use of some of the standard and relatively simple manipulations of matrix algebra we are able to analyze such things as subgroup formations, cliques, and indirect chains of influence from one person to another. The application of this analysis technique to the sociometric data from the Westgate courts yields some important insights into their structure.

PREVIOUS METHODS OF ANALYSIS

Initial attempts at the analysis and description of the exact patterning of interconnections in a group took the form of drawing complicated diagrams where the connections were represented by lines, with arrows on them, between individuals. Such diagrams might, for example, be drawn for the patterns of interconnections within Tolman Court and within Howe Court, as shown in Figures 9a and b. Some things become readily apparent from an inspection of and comparison between these "sociograms." Both courts seem very similar. In each court there are seven or eight people who give several choices among each other and four other people who are relatively or completely separated from the larger subgroup of seven or eight. Also, in each court there are one or two complete isolates who neither give nor receive any choices within the court. It is extremely difficult to determine more than this from inspection of these diagrams.

It is understandable that such a diagram would become unwieldy if the number of members increased or if the number of choices made by each member increased to any appreciable degree. There are no operating rules for such diagrams. One merely arranges them by trial and error so as to make the diagram look as simple as possible and then one further examines it with the hope that he will be alert enough to see what is to be

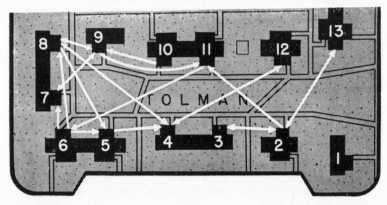

FIG. 9a.   Pattern of Sociometric Connections in Tolman Court

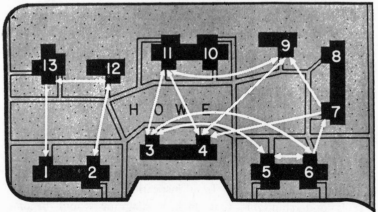

FIG. 9b.   Pattern of Sociometric Connections in Howe Court

seen. The differences between these two courts, which we shall later clearly show to exist, are difficult to perceive in these diagrams. Indeed, we were not aware of them until the sociometric patterns were subjected to a more systematic and rigorous form of analysis.

It was the recognition of these difficulties that led Northway[1] and Cook[2] to attempt to formulate a system which would order the sociometric diagram so as to make it more easily understandable. These attempts, however, still left the analysis of sociometric patterns in a vague and relatively unsystematic state. A large step forward was taken by Forsyth and Katz[3] in suggesting the use of a matrix and some of the manipulations of matrix algebra for the analysis of sociometric patterns. Their idea was to represent the sociometric pattern in a matrix form and then to rearrange this matrix, according to certain principles, in order to have it reveal what subgroupings were present. Figure 10a shows the representation of the sociometric pattern of Tolman Court in matrix form and Figure 10b shows the result of the consequent rearrangement manipulations of this matrix. The matrix presentation is simply performed by listing the individuals in the group along the rows and along the columns in the same order. The choices that any individual makes are then indicated by the number 1, in one of the squares, so that the row corresponds to the person making the choice and the column corresponds to the person receiving the choice. The squares along the main diagonal of the matrix are, of course, left blank, since individuals did not choose themselves. Looking across any row reveals

[1] Northway, M. L., "A Method for Depicting Social Relationships Obtained by Sociometric Testing," *Sociometry*. Vol. 3, pp. 144-150, 1940.

[2] Cook, L. A., "An Experimental Sociographic Study of a Stratified 10th Grade Class," *American Sociological Review*. Vol. 10, pp. 250-261, 1945.

[3] Forsyth, E., and Katz, L., "A Matrix Approach to the Analysis of Sociometric Data: Preliminary Report," *Sociometry*. Vol. 9, pp. 340-347, 1946.

who was chosen by that person and looking down any column reveals from whom that person received choices.

The presentation in this form offers little advantage over the more complicated sociometric diagram for direct inspection. Some manipulations of the matrix, however, tend to simplify

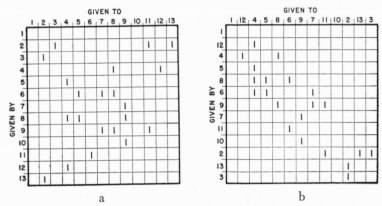

a   b

FIG. 10a.   Matrix Presentation of Sociometric Pattern in Tolman Court
FIG. 10b.   Canonical Matrix Presentation of Sociometric Pattern in Tolman Court

it. The suggestion of Forsyth and Katz is to rearrange the order of the members of the group so that the numbers in the matrix cluster are as close as possible along the diagonal. More technically, they suggest rearranging the order of the rows and columns so as to minimize the square of the perpendicular deviations of the numbers from the diagonal of the matrix. This rearrangement will show, clustered together, those people who choose each other frequently and, relatively separated, those who do not choose each other. Thus, in Figure 10b we can see which individuals in the group cluster together and which are far apart. This enables us to separate subgroups, and would seem to be a plausible means of analyzing changes in the pattern of connections in a group from one time to another. It does not, however, seem to be too helpful a method for comparing two different groups, and the labor involved in obtaining the ordering of the matrix which will cluster the choices most closely along the diagonal is quite tedious.

MEASURES OF THE PATTERN OF INTERCONNECTIONS

Before considering the methods of matrix manipulation which can satisfactorily handle these problems, let us examine briefly the kinds of measures of the patterns of interconnections which seem valuable to us and which these matrix manipulations will yield.

1. *Two-step indirect connections among people:* If we deal with the concept of a social structure or a group, rather than with relationships between pairs of people, the one-step connections between people (direct choices which they make) are clearly inadequate for a full description. The social group in which a person moves extends beyond his immediate friends. It also extends to the friends of these friends. These indirect connections are thus two-step ones. The character and behavior of the immediate group will depend in part upon these indirect connections. The way influence or information spreads through a structure will also be determined by such indirect connections. The exact determination of all such indirect two-step connections among people can be simply determined by matrix multiplication.

2. *Three-step or more indirect connections:* The same meanings and importances which apply to two-step connections logically apply to more indirect chains of connection among people. By matrix multiplication, it is possible to determine in simple, non-trial-and-error fashion all the chains by which influence or communication might spread through a group.

3. *Tendencies toward subgroup formation:* A major dimension on which groups may differ from one another is the extent to which the total group is structured into subgroups. Finding

such subgroups necessitates looking at the interrelations among a number of people. As will be seen later, by means of the same matrix multiplications which show us the existence of chains of indirect connections, we may also determine clearly and unequivocally the existence of various degrees of subgrouping.

THE METHOD OF MATRIX MULTIPLICATION

When the sociometric pattern is presented in a matrix form, an analysis of some aspects of the structure of the group can be performed by the relatively simple means of squaring and cubing this matrix.[4] Let us follow through these operations to see how they are performed and what type of information they will yield. In Figure 11a are shown, side by side, the original matrices for Tolman and Howe Courts. Figure 11b shows the squares of these two matrices and Figure 11c shows the matrices cubed. The squared matrix is readily obtained in the following way: to obtain the number which goes into the cell designated by column c and row r of the squared matrix, we multiply each cell in column c of the original matrix by the corresponding cell of row r and then add these products up. The cells in any row which "correspond" with the cells of any column are easy to determine. For example, the corresponding cells of the third row and the fourth column are such that if person 3 chooses someone who in turn chooses person 4, this will cause a 1 to appear in the squared matrix cell designated by row 3, column 4. The general equation for this multiplication might be written as follows:

$$A^2{}_{rc} = A_{1c}A_{r1} + A_{2c}A_{r2} + A_{3c}A_{r3} + \ldots + A_{nc}A_{rn}$$

In this equation $A^2{}_{rc}$ refers to the number in the cell of the squared matrix in the r row of the c column; $A_{1c}A_{r1}$ refers to the product of the number in the cell in the first row of the c column

[4] The application of matrix multiplication to the analysis of sociometric patterns was developed together with Mr. Albert Perry and Mr. Duncan Luce of the Massachusetts Institute of Technology.

and the number in the r row of the first column of the unsquared matrix, and so on.

This procedure is carried out through a short cut. The products of the corresponding cells of a row and a column will yield numbers other than zero only if a 1 appears in both cells which

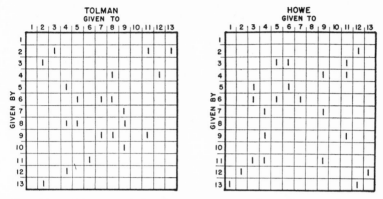

Fig. 11a. Matrices of Sociometric Patterns for Tolman and Howe Courts

are being considered. Thus, a two-step connection where individual 2 chooses individual 11, and 11 chooses individual 6 (as is the case in the matrix of Tolman Court) will contribute a number in the row 2, column 6 cell of the squared matrix. Thus, to obtain the numbers which, for example, go in row 8 of the squared Tolman matrix, we observe that row 8 in the original matrix has 1's in columns 4, 5, and 9. We then look down each column of the original matrix successively looking only for numbers in the corresponding rows 4, 5, and 9. Column 1 has nothing in either 4, 5, or 9 row, nor do columns 2 and 3. Column 4 has a 1 in row 5 and so we write a 1 in the fourth column of the eighth row of the squared matrix. If a column of the original matrix contained 1's in two or all three of these rows a 2 or 3, respectively, would be written in the appropriate position of the squared matrix.

Each figure in this matrix represents the number of two-step connections that exist between the specified two members of the group. Thus the one in the eleventh column of the third row of the squared Tolman Court matrix in Figure 11b indicates that there is one two-step connection from number 3 to number 11. Looking at the original matrix we can easily locate this connection. Number 3 chooses number 2 and individual number 2 chooses number 11. It is clear, of course, that this relationship need not be symmetrical, just as the one-step connections need not be symmetrical. Here for example, there is not any two-step connection from number 11 to number 3.

The numbers that appear in the diagonal of this squared matrix have a special meaning. They indicate the number of two-step connections that exist from a person back to himself, or, in other words, they indicate the number of mutual sociometric choices in which this person was involved. Thus, the number 2 in the fourth row of the fourth column of the squared Howe Court matrix indicates that individual number 4 had two mutual choices. Looking back at the original unsquared matrix we readily see that these mutual choices were with individuals numbers 9 and 11. It is immediately clear in comparing the two courts that while about the same number of people in each court were involved in mutual choices, the number of such mutual choices were considerably greater in Howe Court than in Tolman Court.

The meaning of these two-step connections between different people is quite important. For example, if the original sociometric choice indicates influence from Mr. A to Mr. B, the squared matrix would indicate the extent of indirect influence which Mr. A has and exactly which other people he influences indirectly. If the original sociometric data indicated channels of communication for information, the squared matrix would tell

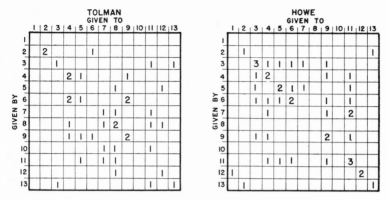

Fig. 11b. Squared Matrices of Sociometric Patterns for Tolman and Howe Courts

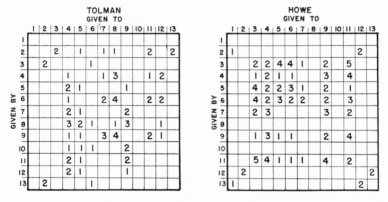

Fig. 11c. Cubed Matrices of Sociometric Patterns for Tolman and Howe Courts

us, for example, that an item of information starting with number 8 in Tolman Court would be heard by numbers 4, 7, 11, and 12 in two steps, and if started with number 12 in Howe Court would be heard in two steps only by number 1. In Tolman Court, individual number 8 could communicate to number 4, 5, and 8 and from these people the information would spread to the others. In Howe Court, individual number 12 could communicate to numbers 2 and 13 but the information would not travel far. Number 2 could communicate to no one except back to number 12. Number 13 could communicate back to number 12 and also to number 1. Individual number 1 would thus be the only one to have heard it in two steps. It is interesting to note that this would be the end of the circulation of this item of information in Howe Court since individual number 1 has no connections with anyone other than 13, his original informant.

While most people in these two courts had more indirect two-step connections than direct one-step connections, there were some who did not. Thus, number 2 in Tolman Court had three one-step connections with other people but only one two-step connection with anyone else. Thus, while communications or influences (assuming the connections imply communication or influence) would tend to spread farther and farther if started with most people; if started with someone like number 2 in Tolman Court, it would probably taper off quickly and not spread far at all.

The cube of the matrix shown in Figure 11c, which gives information on three-step connections, is obtained by multiplying the original matrix by the squared matrix in the same way that the original matrix was multiplied by itself. The formula for obtaining the values of the cells of the cubed matrix would be written similarly as:

$$A^3{}_{rc} = A_{1c}A^2{}_{r2} + A_{2c}A^2{}_{r2} + A_{3c}A^2{}_{r3} + \ldots + A_{nc}A^2{}_{rn}$$

The actual calculation is again performed rather simply. To obtain the numbers which appear in the seventh row of the cubed matrix of Howe Court, for example, we note that in the original matrix there are 1's in the fourth and ninth columns of the seventh row. We then look at each column of the squared matrix to see if there are any numbers in the fourth and ninth rows. Column 1 has zero; column 2 has zero; column 3 has a 1 in the fourth and a 1 in the ninth row and consequently a 2 appears in the cubed matrix; column 4 has a 2 in row four and a 1 in row nine and consequently a 3 appears in the appropriate cell of the cubed matrix, and so on.

The meaning of the figures in this cubed matrix is similar to their meaning in the squared matrix. They indicate the number of three-step connections that exist between any two people. The numbers in the diagonal of the matrix now indicate the number of three-step connections from a person back to himself. The implications of these numbers in the diagonal of the cubed matrix will be elaborated on shortly.

It is apparent that these matrices may also be raised to higher powers to obtain the four-step or five-step or even more indirect connections among the members of a group. If we are concerned with a question such as how many people will hear a given item of information in three or fewer steps if it is started with any particular person, the answer may be obtained by adding together the original, the squared, and the cubed matrices. We can obtain information such as who influences the greatest number of people in less than a specified number of steps, which people are influenced by the greatest number of people and which individuals are only subject to the influence of a few, which people in the group are most indirectly connected to each other and how indirect this connection is, or what proportion of the possible connections among the various people actually exists. Being able to handle conveniently and efficiently these aspects of group structure and patterning of connections should make it feasible to study their effects on such processes as communication, influence, social pressures, and many others.

THE DETERMINATION OF CLIQUES

The manipulation of matrices by means of raising them to the third power can, with complete accuracy, determine the existence of cliques of various sizes and with various degrees of "cliquishness." Let us begin by defining an extreme instance of clique formation within a group and then see how we may determine whether or not such cliques exist in any given structure. We shall define this extreme type of clique as three or more individuals all of whom choose each other mutually. In other words, direct one-step symmetrical connections exist between every possible pair of members of such a clique. Clearly, in order to determine the existence of such a clique we would concern ourselves with the symmetrical submatrix consisting only of mutual choices and not with the complete matrix of connections. If we raise such a symmetrical submatrix to the third power we will obtain all the three-step connections that exist between any two people which involve only mutual choices. What would then be the meaning of a three-step connection from a member back to himself which involves only symmetrical choices—that is, what will be the meaning of the numbers which appear in the main diagonal of this cubed symmetrical submatrix? Numbers will appear in the main diagonal of this cubed matrix if and only if there exists a clique, as defined above, within the group. If such a clique does exist then numbers will appear in those positions on the diagonal which correspond to those persons who are members of the clique. If only one clique exists in the group or if more than one clique exists but they contain different members, then the number which appears in the diagonal for a particular individual will bear a given relationship to the number of people in the clique. If the clique is composed of n members, the number appearing in the diagonal for each of the members will be equal to $(n-1)(n-2)$. We may thus immediately determine from this cubed matrix whether or not cliques exist, who belongs to these cliques if they exist, and how many members each clique has.

Let us examine the cubed symmetrical submatrices for Tolman

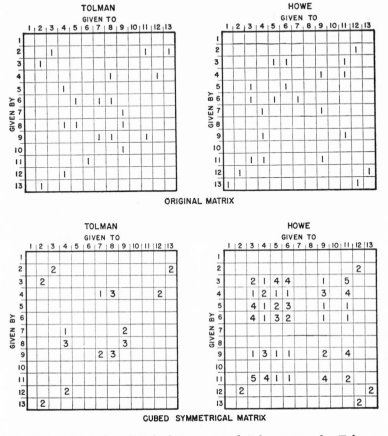

FIG. 12. Original and Cubed Symmetrical Sub-matrices for Tolman and Howe Courts

and Howe courts which are presented in Figure 12. In Tolman Court it is immediately clear there were no cliques at all, since there are no numbers occurring in the main diagonal. In other words, in Tolman Court there was no subgroup as tightly knit as the requirements of our definition imply. In Howe Court, on the contrary, we observe that six people have numbers in the main diagonal and that all of these numbers are 2's. Since the number 2 occurring in the main diagonal of this matrix indicates the existence of a clique of three people we may immediately conclude that in Howe Court there were two nonoverlapping cliques of three people each. We may separate the two cliques very quickly with reference to the original matrix. There we may observe that number 4 chose number 9 and number 11. We consequently know that 4, 9, and 11 comprise one clique and that 3, 5, and 6 comprise the other. Since indirect three-step connections exist in the matrix between the two cliques, we may also conclude that there was at least one mutual choice made between them. Since the greatest number of indirect connections exist between number 3 and number 11, it is highly likely that this is the direct connection. Looking at the original matrix we indeed find a mutual choice between number 3 and number 11. It is clear that these two courts differed markedly with respect to cliques although we found them to be similar in many other respects.

It is also possible to distinguish subgroups which are not extreme cliques. These subgroups may be defined on the basis of mutual choices or on the basis of the complete matrix. We shall give some examples of such more moderate subgroup formations. If we look at the cubed symmetrical submatrix of Tolman Court we see that numbers 3, 2, and 13 are linked together. Here direct choices between numbers 3 and 13 are completely lacking. If we look at the cube of the complete matrix of Tolman Court we find that three, and only three people have 1's in the main diagonal. These three, numbers 4, 5, and 8, are consequently tied together in a circle. Anyone can get back to himself in three steps via the other two. One can, however, only go around this circle in one direction. The best criteria for distinguishing subgroups of less than the extreme degree must still be determined but it is clear that once defined, they may be relatively easily found by means of matrix multiplication.

CLIQUES IN WESTGATE

Table 27 presents information concerning the clique formation in the nine Westgate courts. There are a number of extremely suggestive points which may be made concerning this aspect of

Table 27.—Clique Formation in the Westgate Courts

Court	No. in court	No. in cliques	No. outsiders symmetrically connected to clique	Group standard	No. of Deviates
Rotch	8	0		Fav-active	2
Richards	7	0		Fav-active	2
Main	7	3	1	Unfav-inactive	2
Tolman	13	0		Fav-active	3
Miller	13	0		Fav-active	6
Carson	13	3	0	Unfav-inactive	7
Freeman	13	3	0	Fav-active	5
Williams	13	3	0	Fav-inactive	6
Howe	13	6	1	Unfav-inactive	3

the structure of the group. There were two courts, namely Main and Howe, where the clique or cliques which existed involved a large proportion of the people living in the court. In Main Court, which had only seven residents, the clique contained three people and a fourth person was symmetrically connected to the clique. In Howe Court, which had thirteen residents, there were two cliques of three each who were tied together by a mutual choice and a seventh person who was symmetrically connected to this subgroup. These two courts would appear to be very cohesive courts as was indicated in Chapter 5. They were also the only two courts that had a strong unfavorable-inactive group standard. Howe and Main Courts had only three and two deviates respectively from this standard. The only other court with an unfavorable-inactive standard, Carson Court, had seven people who were deviates. It would then appear that clique formation which involved a large proportion of the members of the court made the court very cohesive and inclined them to react negatively toward a larger organization such as the Westgate Council.

It is also of interest to examine the three courts that had cliques which involved only a small proportion of the residents of the court. These courts, Carson, Freeman, and Williams, seem actually to be split. Freeman Court, with a favorable-active standard, had five deviates; Williams Court, with a favorable-inactive standard, had six deviates; and Carson Court, with an unfavorable-inactive standard, had seven deviates. These were three out of the four courts that had such a high proportion of deviates. It would then seem that the development of cliques which involved only a small proportion of the residents of the court served to make the whole court less cohesive—in effect, splitting the total group.

These data, then, tend to indicate a strong effect of clique formation within a group on the cohesiveness of that group, and on the effectiveness of a group standard which the group may try to maintain. Courts with large cliques were cohesive and had few deviates, while courts with small cliques were not very cohesive and had many deviates. The cohesiveness of those courts which had no cliques was determined by other factors; we find that the four without cliques ranged from highly cohesive courts to courts with low cohesiveness, and from having few deviates to having many. In other words, courts without cliques could exhibit any degree of cohesiveness or effectiveness of group standard, but when cliques existed, they seemed to become major determinants of the total effectiveness of the group.

The dominant influence on the pattern of interconnections among residents of the Westgate West buildings was the division between floors. This division tended to split the building into two subgroups corresponding to the residents of the two different floors, so that there were more connections among residents of the same floor than among residents of different floors. Differences in how much the division between floors actually succeeded in creating separation between the residents of the two floors account for some of the differences in behavior of the residents of the different buildings.

It may be recalled that while all of the buildings were predominantly favorable to the tenants' organization, four of them were inactive. These four buildings had not held meetings to elect representatives to the Westgate Council and the residents in these buildings consequently had little to do with the affairs of the organization. These four buildings were strikingly different from the other buildings in the sociometric separation between floors. While the 13 active buildings had an average of six sociometric choices per building between residents of different floors, the four inactive buildings had an average of only 3.25 instances of residents on one floor choosing residents of the other floor. In other words, the division between floors had produced more of a split in the social structure of the four inactive buildings.

Another distinguishing feature of these four inactive buildings was the amount of contact with people not in their own building. There was no difference in the amount of contact that people living upstairs had with the outside but the people living downstairs in these four buildings received an average of 6.5 choices per building from the outside as compared with an average of 3.2 outside choices per building for the other thirteen. In other words, the people living on the downstairs floor of the inactive buildings had their social life less centered within the building.[5]

It becomes fairly apparent why these four buildings never happened to get together to elect representatives to the Council. Lack of sufficient contact between two relatively separated halves of the building and less interest in the building as a potential social grouping on the part of the downstairs residents made it difficult for such a meeting to take place.

SUMMARY

We have been able to show that one aspect of group structure, namely, subgroup and clique formation within a group, has important effects on the cohesiveness of the group as a whole and the effectiveness of any group action which is undertaken. It will be recalled that in the previous chapter on communication there was a strong suggestion that, at least in one instance, the pattern of interconnections of a clique determined the extent and direction of spread of an item of information.

We have also presented a technique for handling data which deal with connections between members of a group. By means of this technique, matrix multiplication, we were able to determine the existence of cliques. This same technique can be used for determining other aspects of group structure and should enable research on these problems to proceed much faster than in the past.

[5] Both the difference in outside choices and the difference in between-floors choices are statistically significant at the 5 per cent level of confidence, tested on the basis of rank order position of all the buildings. (See Festinger, L., "The Significance of Difference between Means without Reference to the Frequency Distribution Function," *Psychometrika*. Vol. 11, pp. 97-105, 1946.

9

A Theory of Group Structure and Group Standards

SEVERAL major conclusions concerning the functioning of small face-to-face groups have now been reached. The gist of these conclusions may be summarized as follows: In a community of people who are homogeneous with respect to many of the factors which determine the development of friendships, the physical factors arising from the arrangement of houses are major determinants of what friendships will develop and what social groupings will be formed. These social groupings create channels of communication for the flow of information and opinions. Standards for attitudes and behavior relevant to the functioning of the social group develop, with resulting uniformity among the members of the group. Pressures toward conformity to these standards may result in the exclusion of deviates from the social group. Other people deviate because they were never in communication with the group.

It is both valuable and necessary for an understanding of these conclusions, and for making use of them, to develop a coherent theory from which these results may be derived and which can point the way toward further study and analysis of group process. Such a theory, to be of maximum use, should be based on a set of rigorous and well-defined concepts which have unambiguous operational and conceptual meaning. In defining and using such concepts it will frequently be necessary to use in a narrow and specific sense words which have been used in the past to denote broader meanings. This is unavoidable, however, in the development of technical concepts and we shall at various points take the time to define our concepts so that their meanings and their differences from other usages can be made clear.

We shall first concern ourselves with a theoretical consideration of factors governing the development of group structure in informal, face-to-face social groups. Later we shall relate these theoretical considerations to the specific case of the collection of individuals living in Westgate and Westgate West.

The concept of group structure as we use it here is somewhat different and narrower than it has been in the hands of other writers. Among sociologists, for example, it has frequently been used to encompass things like status relationships, cohesiveness, hierarchical patternings, and more. We use it here to denote only the positional aspects of a group—that is, the pattern of connections among different parts of the group.

Among the individuals who make up a group there may be a large number of possible patterns of connections. Two extreme patterns may be easily distinguished between which all other possible patterns will lie. The greatest amount of connectedness among parts of the group would exist when each part was connected to every other part.[1] The least possible amount of connectedness would exist where each part was connected to only one or two other parts of the group, thus resembling a chain where each link is connected only to the one before and the one after it. If a part has no connection with other parts it would, of course, not be a member of the group. The exact number and patterning of these connections will have important bearing on many aspects of the behavior of the group. It is this pattern and

[1] In this chapter an individual member or several members (subgroup or clique) are considered as a "part" of a group. The more general concept "part" is used, however, to leave open the possibility of subdividing group structures on other bases such as roles, positions, hierarchical levels, etc.

number of connections among parts of the group that we denote by the term "group structure."

For different kinds of groups the operational meaning of the connections among parts of the group will be different and may have importance and relevance to different aspects of the behavior of the group. In an industrial setting these connections may refer to lines of authority which would be, at least in part, determined by the formal line relationships which are supposed to exist and would have been determined by the multitude of factors which relate to the formation of such friendships. For the purpose of our present theoretical development we shall restrict ourselves to the friendship referent of connectedness for describing the structure of informal social groups.

Ecological Determinants of Group Structure

One can separate the process of making a friendship (establishing a connection) into two obvious steps. The first step in this process is the occurrence of a contact between two people. The second step is developing the friendship. We shall not attempt to deal here with the factors which determine whether or not a contact, once made, develops into a friendship. We shall for the moment deal with conditions where these factors are randomly distributed through a collection of people. We shall then merely state that once a contact has been made between two people there is a specified probability which governs whether a friendship will or will not develop. Certainly for the housing community with which we are dealing, this condition is satisfactorily met; that is, the probability that a contact, once made, will develop into a friendship is constant for any area within the project.

We shall attempt to examine some of the factors which will determine whether or not contacts will be made. One can distinguish two general processes of making contact with other people. One process is the occurrence of passive contacts, that is, contacts which simply happen. The individuals concerned do not go out of their way to make the contact nor do they exert positive effort in that direction. The other process involves the occurrence of active contacts, that is, the individuals or one of the individuals manipulates the situation so as to bring about the contact. For contacts which are entirely social in nature, the latter variety occurs relatively infrequently. It is relatively rare that one person, on his own initiative, goes out of his way to meet someone socially. When such an active contact does occur it is generally not a direct one, but involves the use of an intermediary. For example, a mutual friend is encouraged to bring about the contact.

It should be emphasized that the relative frequency of the two kinds of contacts, active and passive, which may occur depends much on the ideologies of the people concerned and the requirements of the culture within which they live. There are frequently some conflicts between the two processes. The institutionalization of a custom such as calling on new arrivals in a neighborhood tends to conflict with the strong restraint which exists against striking up acquaintances with new people without having been introduced in some accepted way. People generally hesitate simply to introduce themselves to someone new. It is only after two people have seen each other several times that they will start to nod to each other from a distance and only after some time will it seem appropriate to communicate verbally. This passive kind of contact is probably in most instances the more important factor in determining whom one meets and consequently, to a large extent, with whom one makes friends.

Let us concern ourselves with such passive contacts and inquire into some of the factors which will influence their occurrence. One important characteristic of such a contact is that its occurrence is largely outside the control of the people to whom it happens. The individual is maneuvered by external conditions and his own lack of control enables these external conditions to make themselves felt.

What effect will mere physical distance between people have on the occurrence of contacts in a neighborhood? To the extent that the people living in this neighborhood do not actively seek out others but merely allow contacts to happen as they may, this factor of physical distance should have an effect.

In the ordinary process of going in and out of a home, of working around it, one will occasionally meet others. It is reasonable to suppose that by means of this process one is more likely to meet someone who lives close by than someone who lives farther away. Our hypothesis, then, would state that, other things being equal, the greater the physical proximity between two people, the greater the probability that, within a given unit of time, a contact between them will occur. The average distance between the doors of adjacent apartments in Westgate West, for example, is only about 20 feet. It is less readily apparent, but is equally true, that such small differences in physical proximity will also make for appreciable differences in the probability of a contact occurring. Thus, even in Westgate West, one is more likely to meet one's next-door neighbor than one is to meet the person who lives two doors away.

Certainly not all contacts develop into what might be called a friendship. Whether or not such a further development occurs depends upon a host of factors which might be loosely subsumed under such terms as "liking" and "congeniality." There are, however, at least two ways in which the occurrence of contacts does influence the development of friendships. Contacts impose a limiting factor on the development of friendships in that no friendship can possibly develop unless a contact has previously occurred. Secondly, one may reasonably expect to find a continuous relationship between the number of contacts that occur and the development of friendships in a community. It is likely that, other things being constant, the more contacts one has with a person, the more easily will a friendship develop in consequence.

From these considerations of the relationship between the occurrence of contacts and the formation of friendships we may formulate our hypothesis concerning the effect of physical proximity on the distribution of friendships which we find in a community. If we assume the existence of a community with a random distribution of attractive and compatible individuals (i.e., the probability of a contact's developing into a friendship is equal in all geographical parts of the community), then the number of friendships will increase as the physical distance between the dwelling places of the people decreases. We have thus reached a conclusion concerning the effect of physical proximity on the development of group structure. We may expect to find more connections between parts of the group when we deal with smaller degrees of geographical separation. The exact mathematical function to describe this relationship is, of course, empirically ascertainable. From the data on Westgate and Westgate West described in Chapter 3 one might be led to expect that the probability of a contact occurring falls off exponentially as the physical distance increases. In both projects, the number of friends, plotted against physical distance between houses, would be adequately described by this type of function.

What derivations can be made about how this relationship would change with the progress of time? One may reason that, with a fairly restricted geographical area, over a long enough period of time the probability that at least one contact will have occurred between any two people would approach unity for all distances within the restricted range. That is, a contact for which the probability of occurrence in any one day is low might still almost certainly occur in the space of, say, a year's time. Thus, the relationship between physical proximity and the proportion of people with whom at least one passive contact has been made would be expected to level out as time progresses. On the other hand, there would be no change in the relationship between number of contacts and physical proximity. No matter how much time was allowed to elapse, the people separated by small physical distance would have proportionately more contacts per person than those separated by large physical distances. These two factors, one of which levels out in time and one of which remains constant in time, are the two which we would expect to be related to the subsequent development of friendships. We may then derive that as time progresses in a community the curve of the number of friendships will fall off less and less steeply as physical distance increases. It would be unlikely, however, that this relationship would ever level out completely. Unfortunately there is no good evidence in our data relevant to this derivation. The comparison between Westgate and Westgate West where a time differential in length of residence did exist is confounded with great differences in distances between houses and architectural site plan features.

It is also possible to derive, from these same considerations about the effect of physical distance, something about the number of friends which people living in different locations will have. If we consider a row arrangement of houses or apartments such as exists within one floor of any of the Westgate West buildings, it is clear that the people living in the middle apartment are physically closer to the other apartments than are those who live in an end apartment. The person living in the middle apartment of a Westgate West building is only one or two units away from any other apartment on the same floor. A person living in an end apartment is as many as four units removed from one of the other apartments on the same floor. Therefore, the person in the middle apartment will have more contacts with people on his own floor than the others and will consequently have a greater number of friendships. The data from Westgate West corroborate this derivation. The people living in the middle apartment on the first floor were chosen on the sociométric questionnaire by others on their own floor significantly more often than those in the other apartments. That this did not hold for the upper floor of the Westgate West buildings is due to a complicating factor which we shall discuss shortly.

Clearly, physical distance is only one of several ecological factors which can operate in a similar fashion to affect the occurrence of contacts and consequently to affect the development of friendships. One class of such factors we shall call functional distance. These factors arise from the arrangement and positional relationships of houses, required paths which must be used in going to and from particular houses, common access to facilities, and similar design features. The presence of such functional connections between two people will increase the probability of the occurrence of a contact between them. If, for example, a person must always pass another person's door in going to and from his house, the chances that these two people will make contact with each other is appreciably increased; if two houses face each other the chances of their residents meeting is greater than if they face away from each other; common stairways for a number of people would increase the chances of contacts among all of them.

Such factors of functional distance could act in addition to the factor of physical distance or they could operate so as to tend to reduce the effect of the latter. While it is easy to measure physical distance it is not at all easy to measure and scale functional distance. How can one say what the relative positions of two houses facing each other or a common staircase are on a scale of functional distance? Such scaling would have to be done in terms of observation of how frequently the features making for functional proximity are used. Thus, the relative scale position of the two examples of houses facing each other and a common staircase would depend upon how frequently people used their front doors in going in and out and how frequently people used the particular staircase in question. At present, however, we can compare those people who have a functional connection with those who do not have this connection, holding constant the factor of physical distance. We can, in this way, estimate the importance of these factors in the friendship-making process. On the basis of the same reasoning which we employed in discussing physical proximity we should expect that friendships will be found to have developed along lines of functional proximity.

The data in Chapter 3 provide numerous clear illustrations of the importance of these functional factors in determining which friendships arise. In the upper stories of the Westgate West buildings where all the five residents had to use one of two common staircases, the physical distance factor was found to be less important than it was on the lower floor where there was a separate exit for each apartment. Similarly the residents of the middle apartment on the upper floor did not have more friends than others on their floor in contrast with the residents of the middle apartments on the lower floor. We also find that the residents of the end apartments on the lower floor in Westgate West, who were functionally connected to the upper-floor residents because of the position of the staircases and the placement of the mailboxes for the upper-story residents, were the ones who had made many friends with the upper-floor residents. In Westgate we find that people who lived in end houses which faced the street rather than into the court had many fewer friends in the court than did residents of the other houses. It is clear then that not only the distance between houses or apartments but also their arrangement and design will affect the pattern of friendships that develops in a neighborhood such as this.

We have thus been able to describe two independent factors which seem to affect significantly the occurrence of contacts among people and consequently to affect the development of friendships. It would be well at this point to emphasize some of the implications which stem from the fact that these two factors are found to operate as strongly as they do. The average distance from one door to another in Westgate West is only about twenty feet, and yet we find a steadily decreasing function of number of friends with distance. All the men living in these houses went to the same school and consequently had many opportunities for meeting each other outside the housing project, yet these physical and functional proximity factors operated strongly. We are probably justified in concluding from this that the passive contact plays a rather important part in the development of friendships. The architect who builds a house or who designs a site plan, who decides where the roads will and will not go, and who decides which directions the houses will face and how close together they will be, also is, to a large extent, deciding the pattern of social life among the people who will live in those houses.

What effect do these factors have on the development of groups and subgroups within a housing community? How will they influence which subgroups form, how large these subgroups will be, and how isolated these subgroups will be from the rest of the community?

The formation of friendships is, of course, related to the formation of informal social groups which are a more or less cohesive pattern of friendship relationships among a number of people. To the extent that the ecological factors of physical and functional proximity influence the development of friendships, they will also influence the development of groups. A group will form where there are a large number of friendships in existence.

The heterogeneity of the community, the kinds of people that live in it, and the particular likes and dislikes of various persons will undoubtedly affect what groups form and whether or not groups do form. We will, however, concern ourselves only with the relationship between such group formation and the ecological factors which we have been discussing. These ecological factors will make themselves felt most strongly where the community is homogeneous, as is the case in Westgate and in Westgate West.

The closer together a number of people live, and the greater the extent to which functional proximity factors cause contacts among these people, the greater the probability of friendships forming and the greater the probability of group formation. If a number of houses are clustered together and also face each other, it is more likely that an informal group will develop than if the houses are more widely spaced and stretch out in a straight line or face away from each other. Thus, in Westgate, the court, and in Westgate West, the building becomes the basis on which social groups form. In both of these cases more than half of the friendships which were formed were found among the small number of people who lived in the same court or building.

Groups which form within the larger community may have different degrees of separation from one another. There could be a large number of intergroup connections or there might be virtually none at all. The relative isolation of the group from the larger community will be a function of the discontinuity which exists with respect to the variables of physical distance and functional proximity. In Westgate, for example, where one court neighbors on another court there will be considerable intercourt contact. If each individual court were set off by itself away from the other courts there would be higher degree of isolation of each of the courts.

We can compare Westgate and Westgate West with respect to the continuity or discontinuity of the two ecological factors with which we are concerned. In Westgate West the physical distance from one building to another building is greater than the distance between courts in Westgate. In addition, there is no functional connection between the buildings in Westgate West as there is in Westgate in the form of adjoining back yards. We would consequently expect more relative isolation of the group in Westgate West than in Westgate. We do in fact find that a higher proportion of ingroup sociometric choices were made in Westgate West than in Westgate, and the former showed a sharper drop in number of sociometric choices from inside to outside the building than did the latter with respect to the court. This corroborative result is, however, inconclusive as there also existed a difference between the two projects on length of residence of the tenants, which might act in the same direction.

In Westgate there is no natural division within the court comparable to the different floors within each Westgate West building. From our considerations and hypotheses we should therefore predict that the group formation in the Westgate court would in the long run be more internally cohesive than would the group formation in the Westgate West building. Unfortunately the data which we have are complicated by large differences in length of residence between the two housing projects and the lack of strong group cohesion in Westgate West is more plausibly attributed to the brief length of residence. There is some suggestive evidence, however, on the effect of the separation of floors on the internal structure of the group which formed in the Westgate West building. In Chapter 5 it was found that four of the seventeen Westgate West buildings had been inactive with respect to participation in the tenants' organization. These four buildings had never held meetings to elect delegates to the Council. These four inactive buildings had significantly fewer sociometric choices between floors than did the others. It would seem, then, that in those buildings where the physical separation between floors had maximum effect, it influenced participation in the tenants' organization by affecting the social structure of the group.

It is also probable that the development of groups is hastened by a circular process of meeting new people through one's present friends. Since the factors which affect the friendships of some other person are essentially the same as those affecting one's own friendships, this process should result in quicker and more cohesive group formation in line with the influence of the physical and functional proximity factors.

We emphasize once more that where the community is heterogeneous, one would expect the ecological factors to have considerably less weight than they do in communities where there is a high degree of homogeneity and common interests among the residents.

The Development of Group Standards

The formation of informal social groupings has much more importance for the life of a community than the mere idea of social activities would imply. Wherever we seek to understand the behavior of individuals we must consider the group memberships of the people with whom we are concerned. The informal friendship groups and social groups to which the individual belongs are certainly not the least important of these group memberships. Indeed, they may be among the most important. Certainly it is through the small face-to-face groups that many attitudes and ideologies which affect our behavior are transmitted.

To understand the small face-to-face group as a determiner of attitudes and ideologies it is helpful to understand the development of group standards, the part that interaction between two or more people plays in this development, and the way in which group standards are enforced and maintained.

Before discussing how group standards are formed and the importance of group structure in this formation, it will be profitable to expand somewhat on the concepts by means of which such groups may be described technically. As was the case with our use of the concept of "group structure," these concepts represent a more rigorous and well-defined system for the development of a theory of the behavior of groups. Again, if by our use of certain terms we seem to mean something different from what someone else meant when using those terms, it is an inevitable consequence of the attempt to develop a more formal theory.

One group may differ from another group in the extent to which there are forces acting on the members of each group to remain a member. It may not matter much to an individual whether he remains a member of group A, but it may be very important to him not to be excluded from group B. We shall call the total field of forces which act on members to remain in the group the "cohesiveness" of that group. The force acting on one particular individual to remain in the group may be low and the group may yet have high cohesiveness if the forces in other parts of the group are strong. Perhaps cohesiveness may best be related to the average magnitude of this force in all parts of the group. It is important, both conceptually and operationally, to pay attention to the direction of this force. There might well be a strong force in the direction of belonging to a particular subregion in the group but only weak forces in the direction of belonging to the group as a whole. In this case the cohesiveness of the group as a whole would be quite low.

What are the factors which will contribute toward the cohesiveness of a group—that is, what factors will affect the magnitude of the force field? Two of these can be readily distinguished and conceptualized. One is the attractiveness of the group—the extent to which the group is a goal in and of itself and has positive valence. A group can have such positive valence for various reasons. The positive valence of an informal social group, however, will mostly affected by the extent to which one has satisfactory relationships and friendships with other members of the group. It is apparent that there is a relationship between the cohesiveness of the group and the structure of the group. The more friends one has in a group the more attractive the group will be and also the greater the number of connections that will exist among different parts of the group.

A second factor which contributes to the cohesiveness of the group may be called the "means control" of the group. By this we mean the extent to which the group mediates goals which are important for the members. There are some goals which can only be achieved by means of membership in some group. Such things as status, prestige, approbation, and others are simply the attitudes and behavior of other people toward one and must consequently involve relationships with other people. There are also other kinds of goals which may be made more easily accessible by being a member of a group or over which a particular group has exclusive control. For example, activities such as playing bridge or going to parties may become more easily accessible as a member of a group. There will be forces on members toward a group to the extent that these goals are important for the members and to the extent that this particular group can enable the member to reach these goals. We may then derive that the more valent a group is and the greater the number and importance of the goals the accessibility to which are in control of the group, the more cohesive the group will be.

We may now distinguish another important property of groups which derives from their cohesiveness. We shall call this the "internal power" of the group. A group has the ability to induce changes in the direction of the forces which act on the members, its internal power being defined in terms of the magnitude of the change which it can induce on its members. Groups can induce members to work hard or to be lazy, to vote democratic or not to vote at all, to dress for dinner or to lead a "bohemian" life. Such attempts at induction from the group may come into conflict with forces of the individual member, as might be the case if the group pushed a member to work hard when he felt rather lazy. The magnitude of the change which the group can induce would be defined in terms of the magnitude of this individual force of a member which the group induction can overcome. The magnitude of change the group can induce (its internal power) will be equal to or less than the magnitude of the resultant force on the member to remain in the group (its cohesiveness). If the magnitude of the change the group attempts to induce is greater than the resultant force on the individual to stay in the group (the algebraic sum of all forces acting on him toward and away from the group), the effect would be to have the member leave the group. We may thus derive that the ability of a group to function without breaking up is not only dependent upon the cohesiveness of the group but also upon the magnitude of the change which the group attempts to induce in its members.

Another concept necessary for the description of groups and the explanation of group behavior is the "power field" of the group. It is important to understand not only how much change in force a group can induce in its members but also over what realm of activities the group's internal power extends. This realm of activities over which the group has power we shall call the power field of the group. One group, for example, may have power only with regard to political activities while another may have a power field which extends over political activities and social activities.

We may now begin to define more strictly and more conceptually what a "group standard" is. A group standard may be defined as a uniform set of directions which the group induces on the forces which act on the members of the group. Complete acceptance by the members of these group inductions would result, theoretically, in complete uniformity on the particular matter about which the standard exists. The strength of this group standard and the resulting degree of conformity to it which members of the group do show will be related to the cohesiveness and power of the group. The realm of activities in which this group standard is effective will be determined by the power field of the group.

Let us now proceed to a discussion of how such group standards develop and why they are maintained and enforced. We shall start by considering the function which a friendship has in the development of such group standards in an informal social group. Apart from other aspects of interpersonal relations and implications for behavior, the development of a friendship also implies the development of an active channel of communication between two people. The more intimate the friendship, the greater the range of content which flows through this communication channel and the lower the restraining forces against communication. The opening of such active channels of communication thus means that there will be a sharing of information, opinions, attitudes, values. We may leave out of consideration, for the moment, the determinants of whether a particular item of information or a particular opinion will or will not be communicated to a specific person. It will suffice to say that a wide range of such material will be communicated, and that in a relationship between equals this communication will generally be a two-way process so that the result is a sharing of content.

What are the effects on the individuals concerned of this sharing and pooling of information and opinions? In the case of information, that is, content which is viewed as factual and accepted as such, the effect is clear. Two people between whom such an active process of communication exists will have a common fund of information about a variety of matters. They will both have been, in effect, subject to the same processes of selection of particular contents out of the total range of content which they might conceivably assimilate. In short, they will know and they will not know many of the same things.

In the case of opinions and attitudes, the problem is not as simple and the process is not as straightforward. When an item of information is communicated to a person who did not possess it previously, that item (provided it is really accepted as informational in nature) is now something which the new person, as well as the communicator, possesses. When a view of a situation or an interpretation or an attitude is communicated to someone who did not previously possess this view or interpretation or attitude, it may still not be accepted by the new person. More precisely, it may be accepted merely as information by the new person; that is, the new person may now possess the information that the communicator has this opinion or this attitude. He himself, however, may still have a different one. We must then examine the determinants of whether or not the communication of an opinion will change the opinion of the person to whom the communication is made—that is, under what conditions will the communication of an opinion be effective?

The hypothesis may be advanced that the "social reality" upon which an opinion or attitude rests for its justification is the degree to which the individual perceives that this opinion or attitude is shared by others. An opinion or attitude which is not reinforced by others of the same opinion will become unstable generally. There are not usually compelling facts which can unequivocally settle the question of which attitude is wrong and which is right in connection with social opinions and attitudes as there are in the case of what might be called "facts." If a person driving a car down a street is told by his companion that the street ends in a dead end, this piece of information may be easily checked against physical "reality." He has only to drive on and soon he will find out whether or not the street really does end in this manner. If two people on a hike come to a footbridge across a stream and one of them offers the opinion that the bridge is collapsing and will not hold their weight, this opinion may once more be checked against physical reality. It may require more boldness to do the checking, but nevertheless it can be done.

The situation with regard to social opinions and attitudes is quite different, however. Here there is no such "physical reality" against which to check. If one person offers the opinion to another that if the democratic candidate for president is elected economic ruin may be expected, the second person may agree or not but he cannot definitely check this opinion against "reality." Even if the democratic candidate were elected in the future the second person would have no check against the contention that the resulting state of affairs is economic ruin compared to what might have been. Other social attitudes and opinions are frequently even less subject to "reality checks" than the example we have chosen. The "reality" which settles the question in the case of social attitudes and opinions is the degree to which others with whom one is in communication are believed to share these same attitudes and opinions.[2]

We do not intend to deny that there are many determinants of opinions and attitudes which lie in the personality structure of the individual. We do wish to affirm, however, that attitudes and opinions are to a major extent anchored in the small face-to-face groups to which one belongs. If this group anchorage is firm, then the communication of a new attitude or a new opinion can be readily rejected. Provided one is in communication with a sufficient number of people possessing the same opinion, thus establishing the "reality" of the opinion, one can regard a different opinion as incorrect. Indeed, there will be forces to reject the new opinion since its acceptance would mean moving away from the group in which one has one's "social reality" anchored.

[2] We do not wish here, however, to deny the existence of negative reference groups. See Newcomb, T. M., *Personality and Social Change*. New York: Dryden Press, 1943.

If the group anchorage for an opinion or an attitude is not firm, however, the situation is quite different. Under such circumstances the attitudes and opinions are unstable and fluid and the process of communication proceeds to establish this social reality of commonly shared opinions and attitudes. If a person finds himself in a new face-to-face group the forces acting on him to accept the opinions of this new group will be strong. In a newly formed group there will be pressures to form common attitudes. When a new question arises towards which the formation of opinions and attitudes is necessary, these attitudes will be formed by means of communication with others in the groups to which one belongs.

Among members of the same face-to-face group, then, there will result a high degree of uniformity in the information which members possess concerning situations, and in the attitudes and opinions which they possess towards situations which are relevant to the functioning of the group and about which there is an active process of communication in the group. A gang of delinquent boys will have a different, but nonetheless firm, set of information, opinions, and attitudes from members of a country club set. In both cases there will be a high degree of uniformity within the group, anchored in the "social reality" of the group. It might be equally difficult to change the opinions and attitudes of members of either of these two groups, depending on the cohesiveness of the groups and the amount of communication that normally goes on among members. A change, in order to be effective and lasting, might have to encompass the whole group.

The result of such common cognitive structure, similar informational content, and similar opinions and attitudes, is to produce similar responses to social situations. In other words, there is a resulting similarity in the behavior of members of the same group. We thus have the development of a group standard: the acceptance of a given pattern of behavior based upon a given set of attitudes and ideologies for all members of the group. Once such a group standard has developed it becomes self-maintaining and self-reinforcing by means of the same process which led to its development and growth. It is also able to assert itself on new members who enter the group. The group then induces forces toward conformity since individuals who do not conform are seen as showing behavior which is strange and deviant, and cannot remain in the group without accepting the direction which the group induces.

Even in the absence of any direct induction by the group toward social conformity, the process of communication, by changing individuals' cognitive structure, attitudes, and opinions so that they come more in line with those of other members of the group, tends to produce uniformity in the behavior of members.

For derivations other than the mere statement that communication will produce uniformity, a much more detailed elaboration of the theory of the process of communication is necessary. Such detailed formulation must wait for the further collection of data on the question, but some problems may here be raised and some tentative answers supplied. What factors will determine what is and what is not communicated within a social group? It is probable that, other things being equal, there will be more communication in a social group on matters which affect the behavior of the members in the context of that particular group than on matters which are not immediately relevant to the group's functioning. The direction of the communication flow will be toward those members for whose social behavior the content of the communication is especially relevant. It would tend to follow from this that the strongest standards would be set up by the group in those areas which are related to the functions of the group. It would perhaps also follow that those members for whom a particular area is perceived as especially relevant, would have most influence over the standard which developed. They would figure more prominently than others in the communication process.

It is obvious that there are many other factors which also will affect which members or parts of a group have more influence during the process of establishing uniform cognition and opinions. It is plausible that the number of connections, the position in the group structure, status, and prestige, and the attractiveness and degree of means control which particular members have will turn out to be important variables in determining the influence a particular part of the group will have.

One important theoretical problem is the means by which individuals can maintain attitudes and opinions at variance with those of the group. In order to do this the deviant individual must resist two different kinds of influences. He must be able to resist the changes in cognitive structure and opinions which would ordinarily result from being in communication with the group and he must also be able to resist the inducing forces from the group toward conformity which are set up by the group standard. How can this resistance be accomplished?

According to our theoretical analysis of the effect of the process of communication on the development of group standards, this effect depends upon the existence of an active process of communication in areas where there is no firm anchorage for the existing attitudes and opinions. There would consequently be at least two possible ways to prevent this process of communication from resulting in uniformity. One of these would be to stop or slow down the process of communication itself. Thus, an individual could maintain a deviant attitude by reducing the number of connections between himself and other parts of the group.

The extreme condition here would of course be to completely sever all connections between the individual and other parts of the group, in which case the individual would cease to be a member of that group. Another possible means of slowing down the communication process would be some way of preventing others from perceiving the individual as relevant to a particular area. In this case there would be less communication to him in that area. This might be accomplished by not participating in some particular phase of the activities of the group. Again the extreme condition here would result in no longer being a member of the group in question. Both techniques for slowing down the process of communication toward a particular part of the group tend to move that part to what might be called a peripheral position and perhaps eventually to move that part out of the group entirely.

It is also possible to reduce the effect of the process of communication by making the communication ineffective in the sense of not accepting the opinions and attitudes which are communicated. According to our theoretical analysis this could be done by an individual if his opinions and attitudes have firm anchorage in some other group to which he also belongs. For the resistance to be successful the power field of the other group would have to overlap the power field of the group involved in the immediate communication. In other words, the two groups would both have to have relevance to the area with which the communication is concerned. This might result in successful resistance to the effects of the communication but would probably be an untenable position for the member if the groups' opinions diverged in many areas. He would be in a situation of conflicting group memberships.

The deviant member of the group would also have to be able to resist the inducing forces of the group standard in order to maintain his nonconformity. According to our theoretical analysis the power of the group over this member would depend upon the valence of the group for him and the means control of the group. From this we may conclude that if the valence of the group is low and if the group does not have important means control for that member it will be easier for him to resist the induction of the group standard. It is likely, however, that under such circumstances there is a rejection of the member by the group.

It may be concluded that in all cases within the realm of group relevance the deviant tends to move toward the periphery of the group or out of the group entirely. We may reasonably expect to find that, no matter what techniques of resistance the deviate uses to maintain his deviation and to resist the group influences, he will be relatively isolated from the rest of the group and will have a peripheral position.

It is important to note at this juncture that the similarities of cognitive structure, attitudes, and behavior which we may find among members of existing groups can result from two sets of processes, one of which is described above. The other important process resulting in such similarity among members of a group is the selection by individuals of which groups they will move into, the selection of which people they will have for friends, and with what people they will or will not communicate. There is a tendency to move into groups and establish contacts with people who already have attitudes and opinions similar to one's own. The empirical study of the process of development of group standards, consequently, must be performed on groups which are thrown together without any such selective process. The situation in the housing project with which we are dealing satisfies this condition. The individuals who moved into this housing project did not choose the court or building in which they would reside. They were assigned to houses in rotation, and after the project was filled initially other occupants moved in only as vacancies occurred without any selection on the part of the new residents. Since there was no choice as to which group to belong to, the development of similar cognitive structure, of similar attitudes and opinions, and of similar behavior patterns among members of one court group which were different from those of another court group would undoubtedly be a result of the process elaborated above.

On the basis of this theory of the effect of the communication process on opinions, attitudes, and behavior, one can readily derive many of the results discovered in the Westgate and Westgate West housing projects. Since the physical court structure made for the formation of informal social groups with active channels of communication within these social groups, one would expect that there would be greater homogeneity of both attitude and behavior, with respect to the tenants' organization, within any one court than in the housing project as a whole. It is interesting to speculate how widely this homogeneity within courts would spread in terms of the breadth and the range of attitudes, opinions, and behaviors concerned. This homogeneity would be greatest for attitudes and behavior most relevant to life within the housing project. The effect of the social groupings by courts would undoubtedly be less important as the attitudes, opinions, and behaviors diverge more and more from matters of relevance to life in the housing project. Unfortunately we have obtained no data on this point in our present studies, but this is one of the areas indicated for future investigation.

From our theory we can also derive some ideas concerning the strength of the group standards. The more cohesive the group, that is, the more friendship ties there are within the group, and the more active the process of communication which goes on within the group, the greater will be the effect of the process of communication in producing uniformity of attitudes, opinions, and behavior, and the stronger will be the resulting group standard, as indicated by the degree of uniformity among members of the group and the amount of deviation from the group standard allowed in members. This prediction is also corroborated by the data, in which we find a fairly high degree of relationship between the cohesiveness of the court as measured by the percentage of in-group friendships and the strength of the group standard as inversely measured by the number of people who deviated from the group standard.

It is also clear from our theoretical considerations that if the homogeneity of attitudes, opinions, and behavior results directly from the ongoing process of communication there should be a relationship between conformity to the group standard and the amount of communication that exists between any individual and other members of the group. We would expect greater deviation among those people who have less communication with the group. The data again corroborate this derivation. We find that those individuals who were deviates from their courts, that is, either their opinions or their behavior with respect to the tenants' organization differed from the general opinion and behavior in the court, had many fewer friends in the court.

Since this process of attaining uniformity via communication takes time, it is understandable that in Westgate West, where the residents had only had a short time of living together, there was not a development of any strong group standards. In Westgate West we find lacking all of the evidences of conformity and group standards which appeared so marked in Westgate, where the residents had had a longer period of living together during which this process could go on.

Although the selection of the research problems in this study was guided primarily by basic theoretical interests, we do believe that some of our findings should contribute to a better understanding of the phenomena with which many practitioners must deal. Face-to-face group memberships do play an important role in shaping opinions and behavior patterns. Basic knowledge of the sort presented in this book about the determinants of group formation and functioning, how groups acquire and exert power over their members, and how groups provide satisfactions for their members should throw light on a wide variety of everyday problems.

The finding that accidental contact which is facilitated by physical closeness is an important determiner of what friendships develop and what social groups form is seemingly relevant to a large number of problem areas. Wherever the physical interrelationships among people are subject to change, either by planning or by accident, we may expect changes in social patterns of interaction to occur. Work groups in industry, the geography of the suburb of a city, the allocation of people in a new housing project or new community, the distribution of facilities in a military establishment, all will have their effect on the formation of informal groupings among the people concerned.

The finding that groups have power to impose conforming behavior on members in accordance with the attractions of the members to the group should be of importance to anyone concerned with dissemination of information, changing attitudes, or introducing innovations and establishing new patterns of behavior.

Appendix:

The Methodology of Field Study

THE STUDY of a group in its natural setting has been universally characterized by the great diversity of research methods it employs. In different field studies the techniques of informal interviewing, using informants, participant and nonparticipant observation, sociometry, standardized interviewing, observation schedules, and field experimentation have all been used in a variety of combinations. The necessity for employing such a multitude and apparent confusion of diverse techniques is, of course, inherent in the extreme complexity of the subject matter of the field study—the entire community. These various techniques supplement one another. They gather data on different aspects of the group life and it is only the combination and integration of these diverse data that permits us to construct a coherent and insightful picture of the group under study. The communities we studied and the specific problems we investigated presented complex enough situations to require the use of most of the battery of methodological tools available to the social psychologist.

This section is a description and evaluation of the methodology of the present field study and a consideration of implications that may be drawn from the methodology of this study to that of other field studies. The main points treated are:

1. An examination of the uses and shortcomings of each of the techniques used in this study, consideration of how these methods supplement one another, and of the situational requirements of the field study which make it necessary to employ these techniques in a definite sequence from the more general and descriptive techniques to the more exact and standardized methods.

2. Consideration of the sampling problem in field studies and the possibilities of misinterpretation and misinformation that biased sampling introduces.

3. A consideration of the relatively untried technique of field experimentation, which, supplementing field study, attempts controlled

manipulation of the group variables under study in the group's natural setting.

4. Discussion of the combined use of sociometry and interviewing as a method for studying problems in communication and in the dynamic processes involved in the formation of group standards.

DESCRIPTION AND REVIEW OF METHODS USED IN THE STUDY

A. USE OF INFORMANTS

The chief problems of the investigator in the early phases of entering the community he wishes to study are: (1) to get at the kinds of specific information (e.g., the names of people and the roles they play, the time and place of community meetings, etc.) that will give orientation to the immediate situation existing in the community; and (2) to make extensive enough contacts within the community to provide a variety of sources of information. The usual solution for this problem of gaining a toehold has been to hire, charm, or entice some person into playing the role of informant. The functions of this informant can, of course, be extremely diverse. In the present study we used our informants, a student friend and a typist in our office, in the early stages of the investigation mainly to get the kind of historical information necessary to understand the specific situation and to obtain more immediate information, such as when and where the tenants' organization would hold its next meeting. As we became better acquainted with our informants, we were able also to probe their personal attitudes and perceptions of the affairs of Westgate and of the Westgate tenants' organization.

The strong personal biases of both of these people, however, soon made it obvious that we were probably getting a distorted picture of what was going on in Westgate, and that it would be necessary to establish contact with many more people if we were ever to get a more accurate and objective idea of the situation. We were able to meet some people through these two informants and many more as a result of our attending the meetings of the Westgate organization.

B. OBSERVATION

1. *Informal participant observation.* Though we did not live at Westgate, there were frequent parties, dinners, and informal get-togethers which provided rich and welcome opportunities for observa-

tion of the general pattern of life, attitudes, and personalities of the project residents. We were invited to such social functions by many of the friends we made during the study. Though it was well known that we were interested in and "doing something" with Westgate and the Westgate tenants' organization, such get-togethers were not marked by any special interest in "these persons who are studying us." Relationships at such affairs were easy and informal with no noticeable strain or inhibition in discussing Westgate affairs. Such occasions provided historical information, opportunities for getting group expression of attitudes toward the tenants' organization, and possibilities for more informal, intimate and off-the-record interviewing. They consequently acted as a source of hunches and insights into the dynamics of the community life and presented opportunities for rough validation of previous hunches.

Such observation, however, was possible with only a limited and biased sample of Westgaters. It depended completely on opportunities for meeting the proper people and on personal compatibilities. Since many of our contacts were made as a result of our interest in the Westgate organization and attendance at organization affairs, we had relatively fewer contacts of this sort with people who were uninterested or inactive in the affairs of the Westgate Council than with those who were enthusiastic about the Council. Of the eight couples in Westgate whom we knew socially, six were favorable to the organization and two unfavorable. The six included the president and secretary of the organization and the chairman of two of the committees set up by the organization. Later interviews with everyone in Westgate revealed that only about 40 per cent of the residents in the project were favorably disposed toward the organization.

2. *Nonparticipant observation of the Westgate Council meetings.* The meetings of the Westgate council were open to the public and at each meeting two of our research observers were present. These observers kept attendance records for each court and barracks and made fairly detailed written records of the flow of the meetings. These meetings dealt with all aspects of the community life: complaints, relations with Tech and the Boston community, cooperative projects and entertainments, etc. Records of these meetings furnished a running account of all incidents, projects, and affairs which concerned the community as a whole. The attendance records reveal which courts

and barracks were interested enough in the organization to elect and send delegates to the meetings.

The two methods of observation, of course, supplement one another. Nonparticipant observation provided something of an over-all or telescopic view of the Council and the community, and participant observation a more microscopic view which not only filled in this over-all perspective by revealing individual attitudes toward community affairs but furnished news and gossip which could never have been determined by observation of the Council meetings alone.

Our methods of observation, however, are subject to all of the criticisms that can be leveled at such techniques. Those people whom we observed and employed as informants were not a truly representative sample of the people of the community. Our observations and those of our informants were subject to personal bias and distortion and therefore of questionable reliability. Our observations were not quantifiable. These techniques, then, merely provide the descriptive and historical base for field study and must be supplemented by more systematic and quantifiable techniques if the handicaps of biased sampling and distorted perception are to be overcome.

C. INTERVIEWING

1. *Small-sample, informal interviews.* In the early phases of the study it became apparent that the Westgate people with whom we chatted and spent time were a very limited group. They lived in only four of the nine courts and were probably not adequately representative of the whole community's attitude toward and activity in the organization. Consequently, a series of interviews was inaugurated which randomly sampled some people in each court. Two such series of interviews were conducted within a three-month period. About sixteen people were interviewed each time. These interviews were conducted with a minimum of guidance from the interviewer. There were few specific, predetermined questions and the flow of conversation guided the interviewer in encouraging the interviewee to talk about his feelings and attitudes toward the organization and his reaction to specific events in the history of the organization. In large measure, these interviews were nondirective. The interviewees were allowed to focus their attention on whatever aspects of the organization were of most importance to them. Only when this procedure failed to elicit any information

about certain major aspects of the organization did the interviewer ask specific questions.

These interviews cannot be considered, in any sense, systematic data collection. They were undertaken specifically to supplement data gathered from informants and by observation. Consequently the attempt was made here to interview in all of the nine Westgate courts. Quota sampling was used for these informal interviews. The interviewers were instructed to contact at least one but no more than two people in each court. The selection of the specific people to be interviewed was left to the interviewer except that they were instructed to talk only to people with whom we had no previous intensive contact. These interviews served admirably the function of placing our early information in a broader perspective and of correcting misconceptions arising from the biased nature of the informant and observation techniques.

These three techniques, the use of informants, observation, and random informal interviewing served, then, to supplement one another in providing a reasonably accurate and unbiased picture of life in Westgate and of the feelings of Westgaters toward the tenants' organization. The information gathered in this way was the base and guide for all later attempts at systematic data collection and experimentation.

2. *Standardized interviews.* Data gathered by the observation and informal interview procedures produced a coherent and annotated picture of what was going on in these communities and suggested a series of hunches, insights, and hypotheses which could be verified most effectively by a standardized interview with the entire populations of the two projects.

The interview schedule employed was of the type known as the open-ended interview. This type of schedule is distinguished chiefly by the fact that no ready-made answers are specified for each question. In place of the respondent's being asked to choose between a "yes," "no," or "no opinion" answer to a question, he is encouraged to state his opinion fully. The interview is made up of a fixed schedule of standardized questions. Most of these questions are open, and by nondirective probing the interviewee is encouraged to elaborate, illustrate, or explain his answers.

Customarily, such open interviews have been administered to a sample of the population under study. This is a necessary procedure where the population is very large and if a sample of the population can provide an adequate answer to the problem at hand. In the present study, however, it was both possible and valuable to administer the interview to someone in every household in the two housing communities. Since the interview was designed to gather the data necessary to test such hypotheses as the existence of different group standards in the different courts and the sociometric isolation of the deviate from the group standard, it is obvious that interviewing of the entire population would be most satisfactory. Such interviewing was entirely feasible since our population consisted of only 270 households.

The interview was designed to get information about each individual's attitude toward and his activities connected with the organization, to determine the sociometric structure of the two communities, and to ferret out any jealousies or rivalries existing between the two projects.

For administering the standardized interview we employed six trained interviewers, each of whom had considerable experience with the open-ended interview. The standardized procedure for each interviewer was to introduce herself as affiliated with the Research Center for Group Dynamics at M.I.T. and explain that she was interviewing for a study in housing. The specific questions she asked were the following:

1. How do you like living here?
2. We understand there is a tenants' organization here—
   a. What do you think of it?
   b. Are you active in it?
3. What three people in Westgate or Westgate West do you see most of socially?
4. If a married friend of yours without children had a choice between Westgate and Westgate West, which would you advise him to choose? Why?
5. Would you say there were any difference in economic and social background between people living in Westgate or Westgate West? What kind?
6. How much longer are you going to be at Tech?
7. How long have you been living in this house? How long in Westgate (or Westgate West)?

Only wives were interviewed. The reasoning behind this decision was the following: Since the men were all deeply engrossed in their studies, careers, and part-time jobs, the women of the family usually bore the burden of social life; the women would be easier to contact than the men who were busy in their classes and labs at all hours; to interview the woman in one family and the man in another would almost certainly introduce variables which we could neither control nor identify; to interview the man and woman in each family would have hopelessly complicated the interviewer's task. If the data from these interviews are to be taken as giving a picture of the entire community, it is necessary to assume that the family can be reasonably regarded as a unit and that this unit can be studied by interviewing only one of its members. This assumption might not be completely correct, but in all cases that could be checked with knowledge from informal interviews and observation, the data obtained from interviewing the wife did adequately give data about the whole family unit.

D. SOCIOMETRY

The study of a group in terms of the interpersonal attractions and repulsions of its members is called sociometry. The method of measuring such interpersonal relationships has customarily been that of asking each member of the group under study a question which permits expression of preference for particular companions in some sort of activity. Thus, question three of the standardized interview "What three people in Westgate or Westgate West do you see most of socially?" is a sociometric question.

Analysis of the answers to such questions reveals the pattern of social relationships within the group studied. There has been almost no experimental work on the possibilities of using the sociometric test to identify the channels through which communication and influence in a group flow. It is reasonable to assume that a question such as, "Which people (in a particular community) do you see most of socially?" will reveal who talks to whom and who influences whom, thus identifying the actual paths along which rumors, information, and opinions may travel.

The network of sociometric choices not only allows us to identify the path along which communications may pass but also provides a concrete basis for an understanding of the formation and perpetuation of group norms, standards, or attitudes. It is a reasonable proposition that those individuals who frequently communicate and interact with one another (as measured by the sociometric test) will be more likely to achieve common understanding and a common set of attitudes and values than will individuals who have little contact and communication. This, in brief, has been one of the main theses of this study. The chief use of the sociometric test here has been to identify the channels of communication within the Westgate and Westgate West communities.

In order to test the proposition that a group which is in constant communication will have a common set of attitudes and standards, it is necessary not only to identify sociometrically such a group but to obtain from each member of the group an independent expression of attitude or opinion on some issue of common concern to his group. Questions 2a and b of the standardized interview ("What do you think of the tenants' organization?" and "Are you active in it?") were designed to determine such individual attitudes. This, in essence, is the methodological core of this study: the relationship of group structure and channels of communication to attitudes and group standards on matters of concern to the communities is studied by correlating sociometric and interview data.

The sociometric test, then, has been used for three purposes in this study:

1. To determine the relationship between the architectural design and site plan of these projects and the choices given to and received from people living in specific house positions.

2. To determine the relationship between group structure and group standards.

3. To provide a concrete basis for understanding the paths of spread of the two rumors planted in Westgate by identifying the sociometric relationships of the people to whom the rumor spread.

E. FIELD EXPERIMENTATION

The methods discussed so far (observation, interviewing, and sociometry) have usually been employed in a reportorial or descriptive capacity. They give us a picture, more or less precise, of the situation existing in a particular place at a particular time among a particular group of people. These methods, of course, can do more than describe. Careful study and analysis of data gathered by these techniques can and frequently do point up new relationships among variables.

These measurement techniques, whether used in only a descriptive manner or to reveal relationships among variables, have generally not been coupled with the experimental manipulation of variables. The ideal experiment, of course, is one in which the experimenter is able to contro¹ or match all relevant variables and to manipulate any variable in which he is interested. Such an ideal can, perhaps, be approached in a laboratory situation but only dimly approximated in field experimentation. In general, laboratory and field experiments in social psychology differ in these two major methodological respects:

1. The possibilities for matching and control of relevant variables are far greater in the laboratory than in the field experiment.

2. Manipulation of the variable we are studying is simpler, more easily controlled, and its effects more easily measured in the laboratory than in the field.

These differences point out the major difficulties facing the field experimenter. He is forced to accept the situation as it stands and has no recourse but to undertake an intensive and intimate investigation of the group *in situ* in order to identify and evaluate all variables which might affect the results of any experiment he is planning. Once he has identified such variables he can design his experiment. Only if his pre-experimental studies of these groups have been thorough and accurate can he be confident that his experimental manipulations will be successful.

It is at the stage of identifying and evaluating all relevant variables that such techniques as observation, interviewing, and sociometry indispensably supplement field experimentation. The data gathered by these techniques provide a background and framework for the experiment. Such data, therefore, guide the design of the experiment, the specific formulation of the hypotheses being tested, and the interpretation of the results.

In brief, such a procedure preceded the rumor experiment described in Chapter 7. Data gathered by means of the observation, interviewing, and sociometric techniques provided a reasonably complete picture of Westgate, identified the various groups in the community, and revealed the attitudes of these groups toward the tenants' organization. Such data determined the nature of the rumor and where it should be planted. And it is only by the interpretive use of these data that the specific paths along which the rumor traveled become intelligible and meaningful.

Such a combination of field study and experimentation is a relatively new approach in the social sciences and appears to be a particularly fruitful method of attacking many of social psychology's knottier problems. Not only does field study suggest possibilities for experimentation and direct the design and interpretation of such experiments, but the experiments themselves provide the opportunity for concretely checking hypotheses derived from the field study.

F. THE SEQUENCE OF TECHNIQUES IN FIELD STUDY

Figure 13 is a graphical presentation of the chronology of the study and shows at which points in the eleven-month period of field work each of the techniques was introduced and for how long a period each

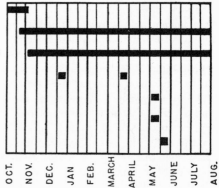

FIG. 13.   The Methodological Sequence of the Study

was used. The earlier techniques were descriptive and personal, the later ones objective, standardized, and quantifiable. Probably some such general sequence as this is necessary and inevitable in all field study. The descriptive, personal techniques orient the investigator and pave the way for the use of the more objective and standardized methods.

The use of such a variety of techniques in a field study has many obvious advantages. It makes possible the collection of a far more complete and comprehensive body of data than any single technique allows. The various techniques supplement each other. For example, by interviewing we collect data that could not be collected by participant observation, by observation we collect information that could not be discovered by sociometry. The data collected by each method help us to interpret all other data; for example, the results of the field experiment become intelligible only when we interpret them in terms of the interview and sociometric data; and since the various techniques explore different but interdependent aspects of the problem, they serve not only as a reliability check for each other but as a means of testing hypotheses derived from data collected by one or more of these methods. Thus, the standardized interview checked the hunches and insights derived from observation and informal interviewing, and the field experiment checked hypotheses derived from interview and sociometric data.

THE PROBLEM OF BIAS IN FIELD STUDY

On entering a new community the field investigator is faced with the circular problem of having to know a good many of the answers to his questions before he can answer them fully. He must make some sort of accurate evaluation of the existing situation before he can effectively design his study. In some way he must gain entrée into the community in order to acquire the necessary information. It is impossible in the process of gaining entrée for the investigator to select his contacts at random. The useful contacts he is able to make depend on his role and position in the community he studies and upon personal compatibilities. Both will, of course, sharply delimit and probably bias the contacts he can make. Customarily the solution to this difficulty has been to put up with the probable bias in contacts with the hope that more accurate sampling can be accomplished when the investigator knows more about the place and the people. This may or may not be successful. Evaluation of its success in the past is difficult because so few investigators have made contact with the entire population of the communities they study, or have followed up their informal observation with studies which used random sampling procedures. These would be the only ways in which it would be possible to evaluate accurately how free from bias techniques such as participant observation and the use of informants have been. Because the present study proceeded from these preliminary techniques to a standardized interview with the entire populations of these communities it has been possible to evaluate exactly how successful the preliminary techniques of using informants, participant observation, and informal interviewing were in making contact with a representative sample of the entire population.

Tables A and B present data on the attitudes toward the Westgate tenants' organization and activity in this organization. These data are given for those individuals who were observed, those who were interviewed informally, and for the entire population of Westgate who

Table A.—Distribution of Attitudes Toward the Tenants' Organization Obtained by the Different Methods
(Percentages)

	Favorable	Neutral	Unfavorable	Apathetic	No. in sample
Participant observation	75	0	25	0	8
Informal interview	67	13	13	7	15
Standardized interview (with total population)	54	12	16	17	99*

* One uncategorized.

Table B.—Distribution of Activity in the Tenants' Organization Obtained by the Different Methods

	Active leader	Active follower	Inactive	No. in sample
Participant observation	75%	0%	25%	8
Informal interview	33	27	40	15
Standardized interview (with total population)	26	23	51	100

were given the standardized interview.[1] Examination of these two tables makes clear the relatively biased nature of the sample we were able to observe and use as informants. This group includes those eight people whom we felt perfectly free to visit socially and upon whom we relied almost entirely for our more descriptive and historical information about the project. Table A, presenting data on attitudes, shows that we were able to observe only those people who had taken a definite stand for or against the organization. Our sample included

[1] Since Westgate West was opened after the study was well under way, there was little participant observation or informal interviewing there. This analysis is consequently made only for the residents of Westgate.

no one in the "neutral" and "apathetic" categories which made up 29 per cent of the total population. The data in Table B, showing activity in the organization, reveal an even more distorted picture. Most of our participant observation sample fell into the "active leader" category, no one in the "active follower" category, and only 25 per cent were "inactive." The trend for the entire population was strikingly different. About half of the population fell into the "inactive" category with the remainder about equally divided between "active leader" and "active follower." Such bias obviously made our original picture of the community an extremely distorted one. This distortion was intensified by the fact that we were unable to obtain even a representative sample of the "favorable" people. Where only 41 per cent of the "favorable" people in the entire population were also classified as "active leader," five of the six favorable people in our observation sample were "active leaders."

Such bias, of course, reflects itself in our early descriptive protocols. It was our definite impression, for example, that there was a sharp and intense cleavage in the community with some people aggressively promoting the organization and others just as aggressively opposing it. Later interviewing made it clear that this was a misconception. There were a considerable number in the community who either knew nothing about the organization or felt completely neutral toward it. In general, the organization was far less of an issue for the Westgate population than for the few people we observed.

The reasons for this grossly biased sample are quite clear. In our roles as outsiders and investigators many of our contacts were made through the tenants' organization. This undoubtedly contributed to the excess of favorable and the excess of active leader people in our observation sample. The reason for the complete lack of people with neutral attitudes or people who were followers in the organization's activities is methodologically important since it is probably quite characteristic of many field studies which use informants and participant observation. In developing contacts in a community in order to learn about certain aspects of the community life, the investigator is most attracted to those people who have much to say about the questions in which he is interested. It is consequently not surprising if, inadvertently, his sample contains extreme cases and colorful people.

The informal, random interviews were introduced as a check and possible corrective for what we thought at the time were the possibly biased impressions of observation. Tables A and B show how well these interviews performed this function. The fifteen people who were informally interviewed six weeks before the total population interview had much the same distribution of attitude and activity as did the whole population. These interviews, therefore, led us to what proved to be a far more accurate evaluation and interpretation of the situation than did participant observation alone.

These data suggest strongly that any field study using an informal observation or informant methodology should be supplemented with some form of randomized interview. The interests and role of the investigator make it very likely that he will be observing a biased sample, and randomized interviewing can serve as an effective check and corrective for possible distortions resulting from this bias.

INDEX

Index